Architecting AI-Driven HRIS Solutions

Scalable Design, Solution Architecture, Project Management, and Quality Assurance for the Modern Enterprise

Architecting AI-Driven HRIS Solutions

Scalable Design, Solution Architecture, Project Management, and Quality Assurance for the Modern Enterprise

Sanjay Mood and Sudheer Devaraju

Published by Amazon Publishing

ISBN:

First Edition: November 2024

About the Authors

Sanjay Mood

A seasoned expert in project management and quality assurance, Sanjay Mood brings over a decade of experience in leading AI-driven HRIS initiatives. His deep expertise in agile methodologies and automated testing frameworks has helped organizations deliver secure and reliable systems. As the author of Chapters 1 and 2, Sanjay showcases his mastery in bridging the gap between advanced technology and practical execution, providing readers with actionable insights into managing and testing AI-integrated HRIS projects.

Sudheer Devaraju

Renowned for his visionary approach to system architecture and deployment strategies, Sudheer Devaraju specializes in designing scalable, secure HRIS solutions. With a strong background in AI/ML integration and enterprise-level implementation, he has successfully modernized HRIS platforms for global organizations. As the author of Chapters 3 and 4, Sudheer highlights his talent for creating adaptable and future-proof HR technologies, empowering readers to build high-performing systems that deliver real value to enterprises.

Acknowledgments

We would like to express our deepest gratitude to **Mr. Giridhar Kankanala** and **Mr. S Amgothu** for their invaluable contributions to this book. Their meticulous reviews, thoughtful critiques, and practical insights have greatly enhanced the quality and precision of our work. Your expertise and dedication ensured that the content of *Architecting AI-Driven HRIS Solutions* remains accurate, relevant, and actionable for our readers.

Your guidance and attention to detail have not only strengthened the technical depth of this book but also elevated its usability for HRIS professionals and technology architects alike. It has been an honor to collaborate with you, and we are truly grateful for your support.

Contents

Preface

Architecting AI-Driven HRIS Solutions is the ultimate guide for technology architects, project managers, and HR professionals focused on building advanced HRIS systems that leverage AI, scalable architecture, and effective project management. This book equips readers with the frameworks and strategies needed to design, deploy, and maintain high-performing, secure, and agile HRIS solutions for today's data-driven enterprises.

Covering every essential facet of AI-driven HRIS projects, this guide is organized into four main sections:

1. Enhanced Project Management for AI-Driven HRIS dives into agile frameworks designed for AI-integrated HRIS, with guidance on structuring cross-functional teams, managing AI-specific risks, and optimizing resource allocation.

2. Testing & Quality Assurance for AI-Enhanced Systems provides a deep look into robust testing strategies, CI/CD pipelines, and automated quality assurance techniques to ensure reliable, secure, and high-performing HRIS solutions.

3. Scalable HRIS Solution Architecture explores modern design patterns like microservices, API-first architecture, and AI/ML integration, all essential for building flexible and scalable HRIS platforms.

4. Implementation & Deployment Strategies for HRIS offers practical steps for phased rollouts, legacy system integration, and post-deployment monitoring, ensuring seamless operation and continuous improvement.

Architecting AI-Driven HRIS Solutions provides the tools and insights needed to succeed at every stage of AI-based HRIS projects. With this book, you'll master the art of creating scalable, secure, and intelligent HR systems, delivering real value to your organization and future-proofing your HR technology strategy.

Chapter 1

Enhanced Project Management for AI Solutions

1.1 AI-Enhanced Agile Framework

The AI-Enhanced Agile Framework is a thoughtful adaptation of traditional Agile methodologies designed to meet the unique demands of AI projects. While Agile emphasizes iterative development, flexibility, and collaboration, AI projects introduce challenges that require deeper emphasis on experimentation, data-centric workflows, and interdisciplinary collaboration. This framework modifies Agile principles to accommodate the unpredictable nature of AI tasks, the critical role of data, and the need for constant learning and adjustment during project execution.

One of the most significant shifts in this framework is the inclusion of experimentation as a core principle. Unlike traditional software development, where tasks have clearly defined deliverables, AI development often involves iterative experimentation. For instance, in software, a task might involve building a login page that either functions as expected or doesn't. In AI, however, tasks like training a predictive model often yield results that vary in quality. A sprint in an AI project might end with a partially trained model that meets baseline performance but requires further refinement in subsequent iterations. This inherent uncertainty necessitates flexibility in planning and execution.

Another critical adaptation is the integration of data-centric workflows. Traditional Agile frameworks revolve around code and functionality, but in AI projects, data quality, availability, and preprocessing are foundational dependencies. Delays in gathering or cleaning data can stall entire workflows. For example, a project aimed at building a fraud detection system might rely on historical transaction data. If this data is incomplete or contains noise, subsequent modeling tasks can be derailed. To mitigate these risks, the AI-Enhanced Agile Framework emphasizes proactive data management, including buffer periods for preprocessing and contingency plans for sourcing additional data.

Finally, the framework supports the interdisciplinary nature of AI teams. AI projects require seamless collaboration between data scientists, engineers, domain experts, and business stakeholders. Agile's collaborative ethos aligns well with this need, but AI-specific adaptations are necessary to prevent misalignment. For example, while data scientists might focus on improving model accuracy, business stakeholders might prioritize user experience or operational scalability. Sprint goals in the AI-Enhanced Agile Framework are designed to balance these priorities, ensuring that technical advancements align with business objectives.

The following diagram visualizes the unique workflow of an AI-Enhanced Agile Framework:

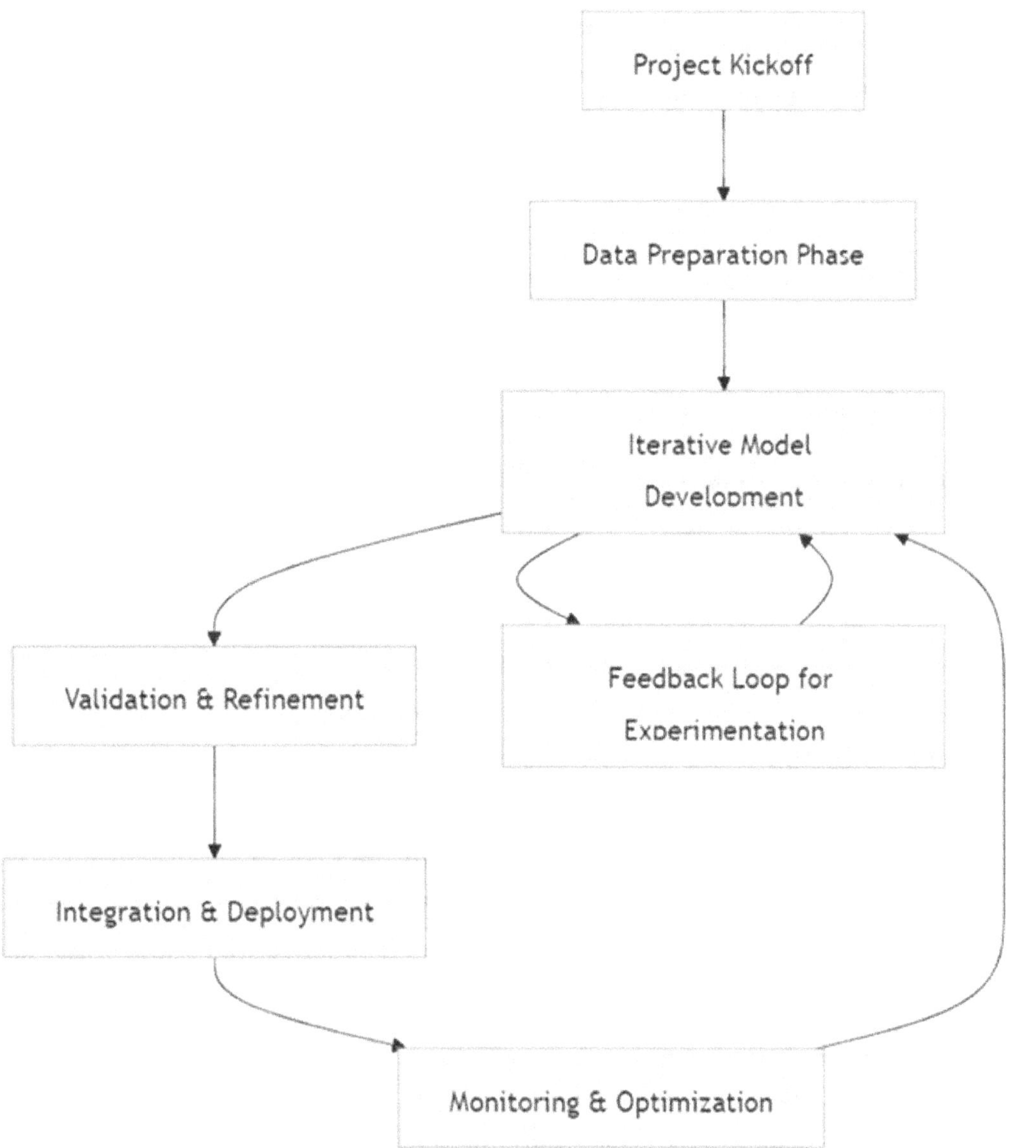

1.1.1 Model-Centric Sprint Planning

Unlike traditional software deliverables, where success is often black-and-white—a feature either works as intended or it doesn't—AI deliverables operate on a spectrum. Success isn't binary; it's measured in degrees of effectiveness. Consider an e-commerce recommendation engine, for example. The goal of a development sprint might be to improve click-through rates by refining the recommendation algorithm. Whether that goal is met, and to what extent, depends on a variety of interconnected factors. Let's unpack some of the most critical ones.

The Role of Data Quality Think of data as the fuel powering your AI engine. If the fuel is low-grade—lacking diversity, incomplete, or riddled with errors—the engine can only perform so well, no matter how sophisticated it is. Imagine training a recommendation system using only data from a single demographic or region. Such limitations constrain the algorithm's ability to generalize, leading to predictions that might work well for one subset of users but fail for others. The key here is ensuring the data reflects the diversity and completeness of the real-world scenarios the system will encounter.

Feature Engineering: The Art of Representation Feature engineering can be thought of as the process of choosing the right ingredients for a recipe. Even if you have the best oven (your AI model), the outcome depends heavily on the quality and combination of ingredients you select. Features are essentially the distilled representations of your data that the model learns from. For instance, in an e-commerce scenario, features might include user behavior data, product attributes, and contextual information like the time of day or season. By crafting features that highlight meaningful patterns—like a user's affinity for discounts or their preference for certain brands—you enable the algorithm to make sharper, more accurate predictions.

Algorithm Optimization: Fine-Tuning the Machine Once the data is ready and the features are well-engineered, the next step is optimizing the algorithm itself. This is where hyperparameter tuning comes into play. Think of hyperparameters as the knobs and dials on a stereo system. Adjusting these settings—such as learning rate, regularization strength, or the number of layers in a neural network—can transform a model from "good enough" to truly high-performing. Additionally, experimenting with different types of algorithms, like collaborative filtering versus deep learning-based approaches, might yield incremental but significant improvements.

A Delicate Balancing Act It's important to recognize that these factors does not exist in isolation. Data quality, feature engineering, and algorithm optimization are deeply interdependent. A poorly designed feature set can't be compensated for by tuning hyperparameters, just as pristine data won't make up for an ill-suited algorithm. In this way, developing AI solutions is less like flipping a switch and more like adjusting a symphony of variables to find the optimal harmony.

The iterative nature of AI development is both its challenge and its allure. Progress is measured incrementally, and even small gains—such as a 2% increase in click-through rates—can translate into significant business impact when scaled. Understanding these nuances is what separates AI projects that flounder from those that thrive.

Defining Measurable Objectives

In AI-focused sprints, everything starts with setting measurable objectives. These are the benchmarks that keep the team aligned and allow everyone to evaluate success once the sprint concludes. Unlike traditional software goals, where success is typically binary (a feature works or it doesn't), AI objectives are more nuanced. They revolve around improving model performance, often incrementally, and are grounded in clear metrics.

Take precision and recall, for example. These are common metrics in classification tasks, like predicting fraudulent transactions. Precision ensures that flagged transactions are actually fraudulent, while recall focuses on catching as many fraudulent cases as possible. If you want a metric that balances the two, the F1-score is a great choice, especially in cases where the data is skewed or imbalanced. For regression tasks—say, predicting housing prices—a metric like Mean Absolute Error (MAE) might be more appropriate because it focuses on how far predictions deviate from actual values.

Then there are business impact metrics, which tie the technical work directly to organizational goals. Imagine a sprint in a sentiment analysis project where the aim is to raise the F1-score from 0.80 to 0.85. That improvement might translate to better customer insights and, ultimately, increased retention. To get there, the team could focus on tasks like trying new tokenization techniques or adding more labeled examples to the dataset.

Prioritizing Tasks to Drive Model Performance

AI sprints differ from traditional Agile workflows in a fundamental way: the tasks aren't always about delivering a finished product. Instead, they focus on exploration, experimentation, and making incremental improvements. Each task is like a small bet—some might pay off with significant performance gains, while others might reveal that a particular approach isn't worth pursuing further.

For instance, **hyperparameter tuning** is a classic example of a model-centric task. This might involve experimenting with learning rates, adjusting batch sizes, or tweaking optimization algorithms. These changes could yield a 3% improvement in accuracy, which might sound small, but in many cases, even minor gains can make a big difference at scale.

Another key task is **algorithm testing**. Let's say you're building a recommendation system. Testing different models, such as Random Forests versus Gradient Boosting or a matrix factorization approach, helps identify what works best for your data. Similarly, **data augmentation**—adding synthetic data or applying transformations to existing examples—can help fill gaps and improve model robustness, particularly in areas like image classification or natural language processing.

Finally, **validation strategies** play an important role. Cross-validation techniques, such as stratified sampling or k-fold validation, ensure the model performs well on unseen data and doesn't just memorize the training set.

These tasks may not guarantee immediate results, but collectively, they drive the model closer to achieving its objectives. And because outcomes are often probabilistic, teams must embrace the uncertainty that comes with this kind of work.

Embracing Flexibility in Sprint Execution

AI development is rarely predictable. It's common to hit unexpected roadblocks—maybe the data isn't as clean as anticipated, or an algorithm that seemed promising doesn't perform well in practice. This is why flexibility is so crucial during AI sprints. Plans are more of a starting point than a rigid blueprint, and teams need to adapt as they uncover new insights.

For example, imagine a team working to improve the accuracy of an image classification model. Halfway through the sprint, they realize the training data lacks diversity, which is skewing the model's predictions. At this point, the team might pivot to tasks like collecting additional data or applying data augmentation techniques, even if it wasn't part of the original plan.

This ability to pivot isn't a weakness in planning—it's a strength. AI sprints are all about learning and adjusting in real time, with the ultimate goal of building a model that performs better and aligns with business objectives. By focusing on measurable goals, prioritizing impactful tasks, and staying flexible, teams can navigate the uncertainties of AI development while still driving meaningful progress.

Scenario: Navigating Challenges in Medical Image Classification

Imagine a team tasked with developing a deep learning model to classify medical images. The sprint starts with a clear goal: train the model on a newly acquired dataset and aim for a measurable improvement in classification accuracy. Everything seems on track until mid-sprint, when the team discovers a significant issue—the dataset is noisy, with many mislabeled images.

At this point, the team faces a choice: stick rigidly to the original plan and risk building a model on flawed data, or pivot to address the problem head-on. Flexibility becomes essential. The team might decide to allocate additional time for **data cleaning and re-labeling**, ensuring the dataset's integrity. They could also turn to **data augmentation techniques** to make the most of the clean examples they do have, generating variations to increase the dataset's effective size.

Another adjustment might involve **redefining the sprint goal**, shifting from producing a polished model to creating a robust baseline for future iterations. This allows the team to adapt without losing sight of the broader objective. By staying nimble, they ensure the sprint contributes meaningfully to the project, even if it doesn't deliver the originally planned results.

Best Practices for Model-Centric Sprint Planning

AI development introduces unique challenges, particularly the need for experimentation and flexibility. Effective sprint planning in this context requires thoughtful adjustments to traditional Agile methods. Here are some best practices for keeping AI sprints productive and focused:

1. Define Sprint Goals Around Performance Metrics

Clear, measurable goals help the team stay aligned and provide an objective way to assess progress. Instead of vague objectives like "improve the model," aim for something specific: "Increase the recall of the classification model by 5%." Tying goals to metrics ensures clarity and drives work that directly impacts model performance.

2. Include Time Buffers for Experimentation

AI development is inherently unpredictable. A hyperparameter tuning task that looks straightforward might take twice as long as expected—or yield no improvement at all. Building time buffers into the sprint plan allows teams to iterate, explore alternative approaches, and recover from unexpected setbacks without derailing the entire sprint.

3. Prioritize High-Impact Tasks

With limited time, it's crucial to focus on the work that delivers the greatest return. For example, improving the quality of the dataset or refining cross-validation methods might have a bigger impact on the model's performance than trying out a new algorithm. By identifying and tackling bottlenecks, teams can maximize their progress.

Example Planning Workflow

Let's walk through how a sprint might be structured using these principles:

Sprint Goal

Improve model accuracy from 80% to 85%.

Planned Tasks

1. **Hyperparameter Tuning**: Adjusting key parameters like dropout rates or learning rates in the neural network to optimize performance.

2. **Ensemble Techniques**: Testing methods to combine predictions from multiple models, such as bagging or boosting, to enhance accuracy.

3. **Feature Engineering**: Adding new features derived from external data sources to capture additional patterns the model might otherwise miss.

This workflow focuses on tasks that directly contribute to the sprint goal, leaving room for flexibility in execution. For example, if ensemble techniques prove ineffective early in the sprint, the team might reallocate that time to further hyperparameter tuning or dataset refinement.

The following diagram illustrates a typical workflow for model-centric sprint planning:

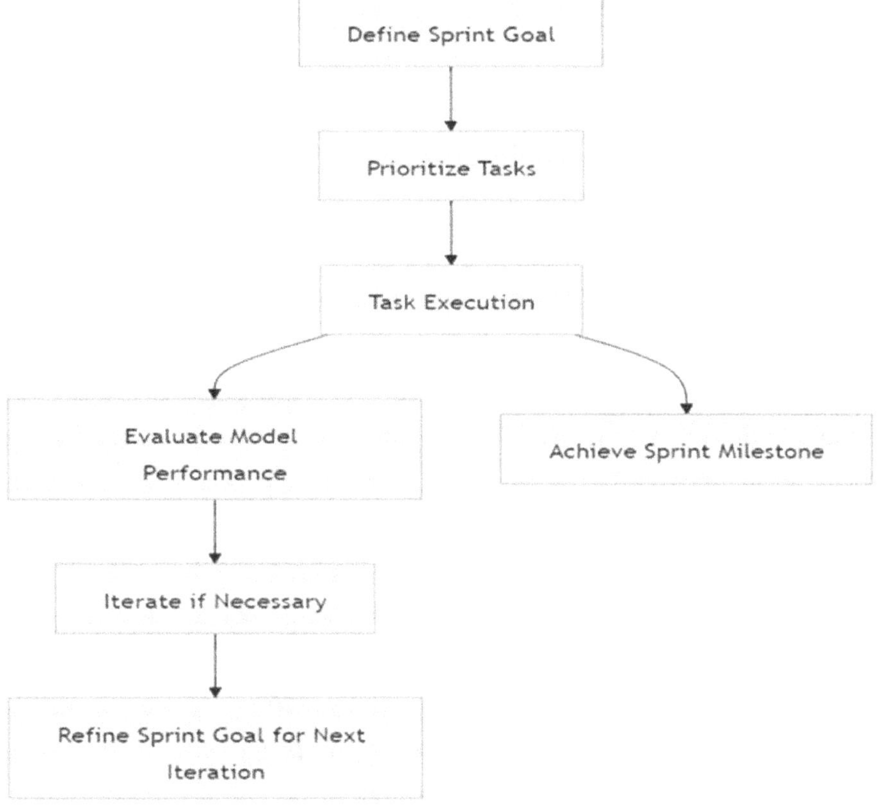

AI development doesn't fit neatly into traditional software workflows. The experimental nature of building models, coupled with the need for precision and adaptability, calls for a different approach. Model-centric sprint planning bridges the gap by tailoring Agile principles to the realities of AI projects. By focusing on performance-based goals, prioritizing tasks with the greatest impact, and staying flexible when challenges arise, teams can navigate the uncertainties of AI development while maintaining steady progress. This approach not only ensures productive sprints but also keeps technical work aligned with business objectives, laying the groundwork for meaningful AI solutions.

1.1.2 Hybrid Methodology for AI Projects

AI projects are unique in how they combine structured tasks, like building data pipelines, with more fluid, experimental processes, such as testing machine learning models. To manage these complexities effectively, many teams adopt a hybrid methodology that blends the best aspects of Waterfall and Agile. This approach recognizes that while some phases of AI development thrive with a linear, step-by-step process, others demand iterative experimentation. The result is a framework that balances stability and flexibility, providing structure when needed and adaptability when the situation calls for it.

The hybrid methodology typically begins with a structured phase, grounded in Waterfall principles, to establish a solid foundation. Once the groundwork is in place, the project transitions into Agile iterations for tasks like model experimentation and refinement. Let's break this down.

Starting with Structured Foundations

The early stages of an AI project often involve tasks that are highly interdependent and benefit from a linear, sequential approach. Think of these as the infrastructure and preparation phases—activities that need to be done correctly before the team can move on to more dynamic, iterative work. For instance, an AI project aimed at detecting manufacturing anomalies might start by integrating IoT sensors into machinery, collecting historical data to understand normal operations, and setting up a cloud or on-premises environment to store and process the data.

These steps are the backbone of the project. If the data pipeline is unreliable or the infrastructure isn't scalable, the entire project risks falling apart later on. For example, a predictive maintenance system for industrial equipment might begin with defining the system's architecture, gathering initial data from sensors, and ensuring that the processing pipeline can handle large volumes of real-time data. This phase benefits from meticulous planning and execution, reducing the risk of bottlenecks when the project moves into the experimental phase.

Transitioning to Iterative Refinement

Once the foundational work is complete, the project shifts gears. This is where the flexibility of Agile takes center stage. Model development and experimentation are inherently exploratory processes. It's impossible to predict exactly which algorithm will perform best or how long it will take to fine-tune a model to meet performance goals. Agile's iterative cycles are perfectly suited to this kind of work, enabling teams to test ideas, learn from the results, and adapt quickly.

During this phase, the focus shifts to tasks like experimenting with different machine learning models, optimizing hyperparameters, and validating predictions in real-world scenarios. These activities are dynamic and fast-paced. For example, a team working on an AI-powered inventory management system might initially establish a robust data pipeline using Waterfall principles. Once that's operational, they could move into short Agile sprints to refine demand forecasting models, incorporating real-time sales data and testing new feature engineering techniques.

Each sprint is focused on achieving a specific, measurable improvement. One sprint might aim to increase the model's accuracy by 5%, while the next might focus on reducing its training time. The iterative nature of this phase allows the team to adapt to new information or challenges, such as discovering data gaps or finding that a particular algorithm isn't performing as expected.

Balancing Stability and Flexibility

The hybrid methodology works because it tailors the approach to the specific needs of each phase in an AI project. Structured, sequential planning ensures that foundational tasks are completed with rigor, reducing the likelihood of issues cropping up later. Meanwhile, the iterative, exploratory nature of Agile allows for rapid experimentation and adaptation during model development. Together, these methodologies provide a framework that is both robust and responsive.

Take, for example, a healthcare AI project aimed at diagnosing diseases from medical images. The Waterfall phase might focus on meeting regulatory requirements, defining data storage protocols, and ensuring the system is compliant with patient privacy laws. Once those foundational tasks are complete, the team could transition to Agile, running short sprints to refine diagnostic models by incorporating additional labeled data and testing new preprocessing techniques.

Navigating the Challenges of a Hybrid Approach

Of course, blending two methodologies isn't without its challenges. Transitioning from Waterfall to Agile requires careful planning and clear communication. Teams need to establish checkpoints to ensure they're ready to shift from one phase to the next. For example, before moving from infrastructure setup to model experimentation, the team might review whether the data pipeline is fully operational and whether all required datasets have been validated.

Another potential challenge is managing stakeholder expectations. Different stakeholders might favor one methodology over the other, creating tension if the rationale for the hybrid approach isn't clearly communicated. To mitigate this, it's important to involve stakeholders early in the planning process, explaining how each methodology supports different aspects of the project and ensures overall success.

A Unified Framework for AI Success

The hybrid methodology provides a pragmatic approach to managing AI projects, combining the structured reliability of Waterfall with the iterative adaptability of Agile. By starting with a stable foundation and transitioning to flexible experimentation, teams can tackle the diverse challenges of AI development with confidence. This approach not only ensures technical robustness but also keeps the project aligned with evolving business needs, making it an essential framework for delivering impactful AI solutions.

The following diagram illustrates the phased workflow of the hybrid methodology:

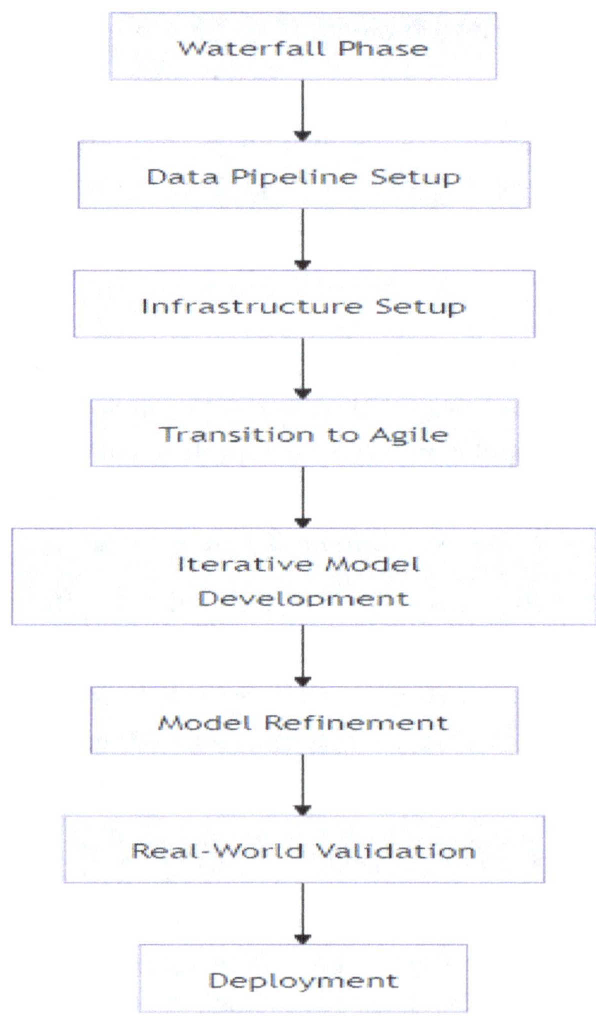

The hybrid methodology strikes a balance between the structured planning of Waterfall and the iterative flexibility of Agile. By leveraging Waterfall for foundational tasks and Agile for experimentation and refinement, this approach provides the structure and adaptability needed to manage the complexities of AI projects. Teams can ensure that each phase of development is optimized, enabling them to deliver reliable, high-performing AI solutions that align with both technical and business objectives.

1.1.3 Sprint Structure for Data & Model Development

AI projects stand apart from traditional software development because of the intricate relationship between data preparation and model development. These two processes follow distinct timelines and deliverables, yet they are so deeply interdependent that progress in one often hinges on the other. To navigate this complexity, a dual-track sprint structure can be invaluable. This approach separates work into two parallel tracks—one focused on preparing data and the other on developing models—while maintaining regular synchronization points to ensure alignment. By doing so, teams can manage both workflows effectively, keeping the project moving forward without bottlenecks.

The Dual-Track Sprint Structure

The dual-track sprint structure recognizes that data and models evolve hand-in-hand. The data track ensures that high-quality, well-prepared datasets are available, while the model track focuses on building and refining the AI system itself. These tracks run simultaneously, allowing for continuous progress, but they converge at key moments to ensure the outputs of one track seamlessly support the goals of the other.

Preparing High-Quality Inputs in the Data Track

Data is the lifeblood of any AI project, and the data track ensures that this lifeblood is clean, consistent, and ready for use. Preparing data isn't just a preliminary step—it's an ongoing process that involves cleaning, transforming, and engineering features to maximize the model's potential.

Take, for example, a sales forecasting project. The data track might begin with cleaning up missing or inconsistent entries, such as filling in gaps for certain product categories or standardizing date formats across records. From there, the team might move on to data transformation, converting raw information into a format the model can use effectively. In a healthcare AI project, this could mean normalizing values like blood pressure or glucose levels to ensure consistency across samples. Finally, feature engineering adds another layer of refinement, focusing on creating or selecting variables that enhance model performance. For instance, in a natural language processing (NLP) project, this might involve preprocessing text by removing unnecessary elements, standardizing terms, and generating embeddings like Word2Vec or BERT to capture semantic meaning.

In practice, consider an NLP chatbot project. The data track would likely begin by preprocessing conversational datasets—tokenizing sentences, removing punctuation, and cleaning up irrelevant symbols. The team might then augment the dataset by adding paraphrased text, making the chatbot more robust in understanding variations of user input. Once the data is ready, it feeds directly into the model track, where it becomes the foundation for training and evaluation.

Developing and Validating Models in the Model Track

While the data team works on preparing high-quality inputs, the model track focuses on the iterative process of building, testing, and refining machine learning models. This track thrives on experimentation and optimization, as teams work to identify the best-performing algorithms and fine-tune their configurations to meet the project's objectives.

Imagine a team tasked with developing a fraud detection system. The model track might begin by testing various algorithms—Random Forest, Gradient Boosting, or a neural network—to determine which is most effective for the problem at hand. Once a promising model is selected, hyperparameter tuning comes into play. This involves adjusting elements like learning rates or the number of layers in a neural network to find the sweet spot that maximizes performance. Finally, model validation ensures the system can generalize effectively to unseen data.

Returning to the NLP chatbot example, the model track might involve fine-tuning a transformer-based model like GPT on preprocessed conversational data. The team could validate the model by comparing its performance against benchmark datasets, checking metrics such as response accuracy or fluency. Once the model meets these standards, an initial version could be deployed in a test environment to gather user feedback, closing the loop for further refinement.

Synchronizing Data and Model Development

Even though the data and model tracks operate independently, they are deeply interconnected. Regular synchronization points are built into the sprint structure to ensure that both tracks align seamlessly. These checkpoints create opportunities for collaboration, where insights from one track inform decisions in the other.

For instance, a data team might hand off newly engineered features—such as customer demographic data enriched with geographic insights—to the model team for training and evaluation. Conversely, the model team might provide feedback about gaps or inconsistencies in the dataset. If a fraud detection model struggles to identify specific transaction patterns, the data team might focus on augmenting the dataset with additional examples of similar fraud types. Joint review meetings between the two teams further ensure that everyone is on the same page, addressing challenges collaboratively and planning next steps with a unified vision.

Consider a predictive maintenance project for industrial equipment. The data track might preprocess sensor data, extracting features like vibration frequency and temperature trends. Meanwhile, the model track trains a neural network on these features, only to discover that performance suffers due to missing data for certain types of equipment. This insight feeds back into the data track, prompting the team to source additional sensor readings or generate synthetic data to fill the gaps.

The Benefits of Dual-Track Sprints

The dual-track approach offers a practical way to manage the complexities of AI development. By allowing data preparation and model development to progress in parallel, teams can avoid unnecessary delays and make steady progress on both fronts.

One of the biggest advantages is the ability to work simultaneously on foundational and experimental tasks. For instance, while the data team cleans and transforms historical sales data, the model team can experiment with baseline algorithms using smaller subsets of the dataset. This parallel progress keeps the project moving, reducing the risk of one track becoming a bottleneck for the other.

Another benefit is the feedback loop created between tracks. Insights from the model team—such as a need for more diverse examples—can directly inform the data team's priorities, leading to more informed and effective iterations. For example, if a churn prediction model struggles with certain customer segments, the data team might augment the dataset with additional representative samples, allowing the model team to refine their approach.

Managing Complexity with Structure and Collaboration

The dual-track sprint structure is more than just a way to organize tasks; it's a framework for managing the intricate relationship between data and models in AI projects. By balancing independence with regular synchronization, teams can maintain momentum on both tracks while ensuring that their efforts are aligned. This approach not only enhances efficiency but also fosters a collaborative environment where every iteration builds on the last, bringing the project closer to delivering impactful results.

The following diagram illustrates how the Data Track and Model Track operate in parallel, with synchronization points ensuring alignment:

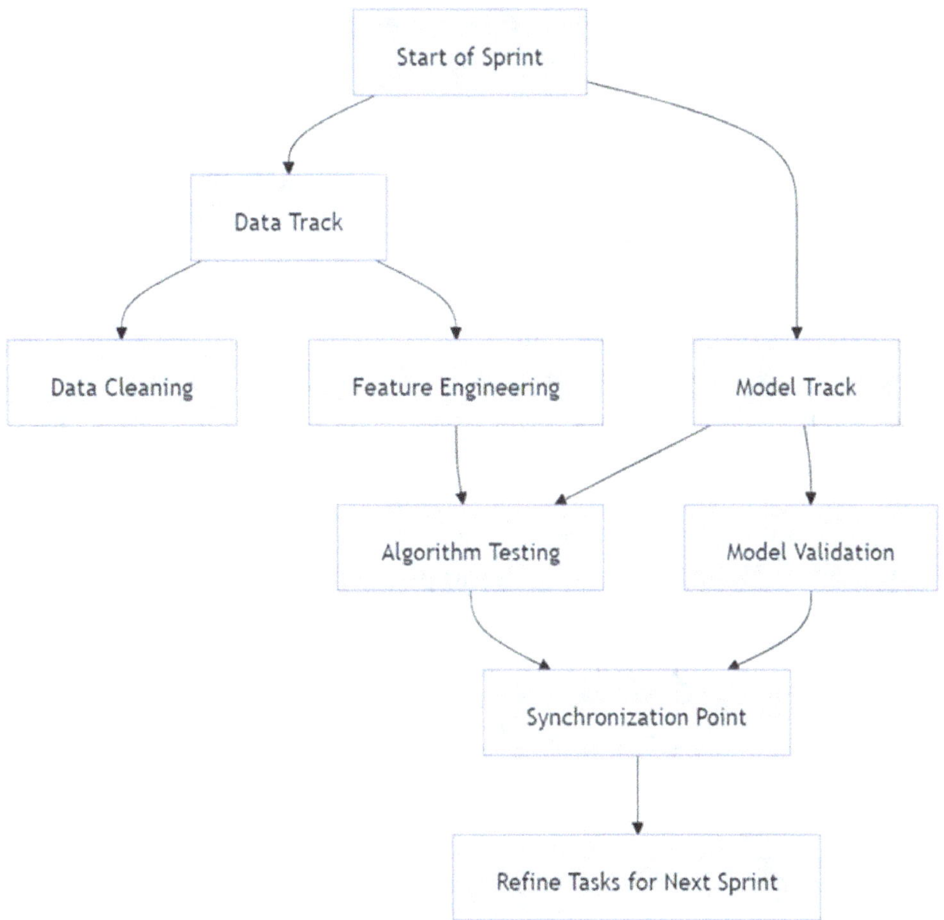

The dual-track sprint structure is a powerful approach for managing the parallel workflows of data preparation and model development in AI projects. By enabling parallel progress and fostering informed iterations, this methodology ensures that both tracks contribute effectively to the sprint goals. Synchronization points further enhance collaboration, aligning efforts and addressing dependencies between tracks. This structured yet flexible approach is essential for navigating the complexities of AI development, ensuring that teams can deliver high-quality solutions on schedule.

1.2 Team Structure & Roles

AI projects are inherently collaborative, requiring seamless integration of expertise from various domains to address their unique complexities. Unlike traditional software development projects, where roles are often clearly defined and segmented, AI initiatives demand a harmonious blend of technical acumen, domain-specific insights, and operational precision. This interdisciplinary approach is necessitated by the multifaceted nature of AI workflows, which involve handling large and diverse datasets, designing sophisticated algorithms, and ensuring that outputs align with practical, real-world applications.

The success of an AI project hinges on assembling a multidisciplinary team with complementary skill sets. These teams typically include data scientists, machine learning (ML) engineers, domain experts, software developers, project managers, and business stakeholders. Each role brings unique value, ensuring that the project is not only technically robust but also practically viable and aligned with the organization's strategic objectives. For instance, data scientists are responsible for developing and fine-tuning models, while domain experts validate these models to ensure they are relevant and useful within their specific industry, such as healthcare, finance, or manufacturing.

The Critical Role of Multidisciplinary Collaboration

AI projects are inherently complex, requiring the seamless integration of diverse workflows that span data collection, preprocessing, model development, testing, and deployment. These workflows do not occur in isolation; they rely on expertise from a wide range of disciplines to succeed. Collaboration is not just helpful in AI—it's essential. By bringing together specialists from data science, engineering, business, and domain-specific fields, organizations can ensure their AI solutions are both technically robust and aligned with real-world needs.

At the heart of this collaboration is the recognition that each discipline contributes something unique to the AI development process. Domain experts, for example, ensure that the data used to train models is both accurate and relevant. In a retail-focused AI project, a marketing specialist might help refine customer segmentation criteria, ensuring the model targets the right audience. Meanwhile, engineers focus on building scalable systems that can handle the complexities of real-world deployment, like creating a chatbot capable of managing thousands of simultaneous customer queries without lag. At the same time, business stakeholders bridge the gap between technical work and organizational goals, setting clear metrics for success—whether that's reducing costs, increasing revenue, or improving operational efficiency.

Challenges in Building Collaborative AI Teams

Despite its importance, collaboration in AI is not without its challenges. Multidisciplinary teams often face skill gaps, communication barriers, and misaligned priorities, all of which can slow progress or derail projects if not addressed.

One of the biggest hurdles is the specialized expertise required for many AI projects. Teams may need deep learning specialists, regulatory experts, or engineers familiar with emerging technologies like edge computing. Identifying and addressing these gaps can be time-intensive, especially in industries where AI talent is in high demand.

Even when the right people are in the room, effective communication is not guaranteed. Each discipline has its own language, and misunderstandings can arise when technical jargon meets unfamiliar ears. A data scientist discussing "gradient descent optimization" might unintentionally alienate a business stakeholder, just as a marketer's focus on "customer personas" might not resonate with the engineers tasked with building the backend system. These miscommunications can create friction, slow down decision-making, and lead to confusion about project goals.

Finally, misaligned objectives can pose a significant challenge. Technical teams often prioritize achieving high model accuracy or experimenting with cutting-edge techniques, while business stakeholders may be more focused on meeting tight deadlines or addressing immediate market demands. Without clear alignment, these competing priorities can result in wasted effort or unfinished solutions.

Fostering Effective Collaboration

Overcoming these challenges requires intentional strategies to align teams, clarify roles, and promote communication. One of the most important steps is to define clear roles and responsibilities from the outset. Each team member should understand not only what they're accountable for but also how their work fits into the larger picture. For instance, data scientists might focus on feature engineering and model experimentation, while engineers handle deployment and scalability, and domain experts validate whether the solution aligns with real-world needs. This clarity minimizes overlap and ensures everyone has a clear sense of purpose.

Equally important is establishing shared goals that balance technical performance with business outcomes. AI projects are at their best when technical innovation is tied directly to measurable value. For example, an AI-powered fraud detection system might set a dual goal: achieving 90% detection accuracy while minimizing false positives to avoid disrupting legitimate transactions. This balance ensures that technical efforts serve broader organizational objectives, creating solutions that are both innovative and practical.

Collaboration tools and practices also play a critical role in keeping teams aligned. Regular meetings, visual task boards, and cross-functional workshops help foster open communication and reduce silos. For instance, in a healthcare AI project, weekly meetings between doctors, data scientists, and engineers might address issues like model interpretability and regulatory compliance, ensuring that every perspective is considered. These practices build trust and understanding, laying the foundation for smoother collaboration.

The Transformative Power of Multidisciplinary Teams

When done well, collaboration in AI projects is more than just a means to an end; it's a catalyst for innovation. By combining diverse perspectives and skill sets, organizations can tackle problems in ways that no single discipline could achieve on its own.

Consider a team developing an AI-powered fraud detection system. Data scientists design predictive models, leveraging their algorithmic expertise to identify anomalies. Fraud investigators bring operational insights, highlighting patterns that might not be obvious in the data. Engineers, in turn, ensure the model integrates seamlessly into transaction monitoring systems, handling real-time inputs without sacrificing performance. Together, these professionals create a solution that not only identifies fraud but does so in a way that aligns with the organization's workflows and goals.

The benefits of this collaborative approach extend far beyond individual projects. Organizations that excel at fostering teamwork and leveraging diverse expertise are better positioned to harness AI's transformative potential. They become more innovative, more adaptable, and better equipped to deliver solutions that drive long-term value.

Collaboration is not just a nice-to-have in AI—it's a competitive advantage. By investing in multidisciplinary teams and fostering an environment where diverse voices can thrive, organizations set themselves up for success, creating AI solutions that are as practical as they are cutting-edge.

The following diagram illustrates the interplay between different roles in a multidisciplinary AI team:

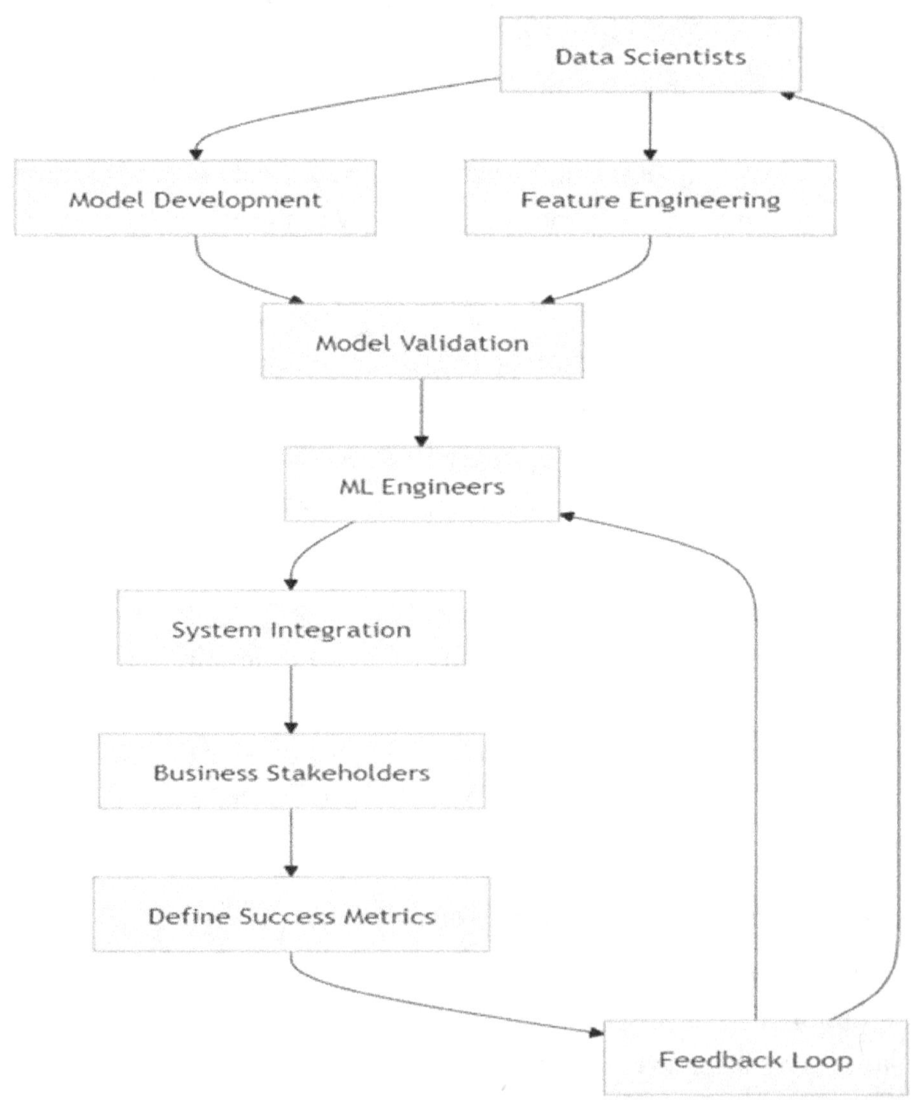

Building a strong team structure and fostering effective collaboration are essential for the success of AI projects. By integrating diverse expertise, aligning goals, and promoting open communication, organizations can unlock the full potential of their AI initiatives. Multidisciplinary collaboration ensures that AI solutions are not only technically advanced but also practically relevant and aligned with business objectives. In this way, organizations can drive meaningful innovation and create lasting impact in their industries.

1.2.1 Cross-Functional Teams (Data Scientists, Engineers, Domain Experts)

AI projects thrive on diversity—not just in data but in expertise. Unlike traditional software development, where roles often exist in silos and focus narrowly on technical tasks, AI development is a multifaceted endeavor. It demands active, ongoing collaboration across disciplines to navigate the complex workflows involved in data collection, model development, deployment, and monitoring. Cross-functional teams bring together specialists from varied backgrounds, creating a dynamic synergy that ensures solutions are technically sound, practically applicable, and aligned with business objectives.

The beauty of cross-functional teams lies in their ability to address challenges from multiple perspectives. Data scientists, engineers, and domain experts each bring unique skills and insights to the table, working together to solve problems that no single discipline could tackle alone. This collaborative approach ensures that AI solutions are not just innovative but also grounded in real-world needs.

The Unique Contributions of Data Scientists

Data scientists are at the core of AI development. Think of them as the architects who design and refine the models that drive AI systems. Their work revolves around uncovering patterns in data, crafting algorithms to solve specific problems, and continuously iterating to improve model performance. This requires a blend of statistical expertise, programming skills, and domain knowledge.

A crucial aspect of their role is experimentation. Data scientists rarely have a one-size-fits-all solution to a problem. For instance, in a marketing campaign, they might test collaborative filtering, decision trees, and neural networks to determine which approach best predicts customer preferences. Along the way, they engineer features—transforming raw data into inputs that make models more effective. In a customer behavior project, this might involve analyzing clickstream data to generate insights into purchasing patterns.

Beyond the technical work, data scientists often act as translators, bridging the gap between raw data and business objectives. In a healthcare project, for example, they might collaborate with clinicians to develop a diagnostic model for rare diseases. Their job isn't just to ensure the model works but to make its predictions interpretable and actionable, building trust with doctors who will rely on the system in critical decision-making.

The Operational Expertise of Engineers

If data scientists are the architects, engineers are the builders who bring AI systems to life. Their role goes far beyond writing code; they ensure that models are production-ready, scalable, and seamlessly integrated into real-world workflows. Engineers are the ones who take experimental models and turn them into robust, reliable systems.

A key part of this process is designing deployment pipelines—automated workflows that take models from development to production environments. For example, engineers might use tools like Docker to containerize a model or Kubernetes to ensure it scales to handle thousands of simultaneous requests. They also focus on performance optimization, making sure the system meets critical requirements like low latency and high throughput.

Consider an autonomous vehicle project. While data scientists might develop the models for object detection and route planning, engineers embed those models into onboard systems that can process data in real-time. Their work ensures that the vehicle not only recognizes objects but responds instantly and reliably, even in high-stakes situations like avoiding collisions or navigating around obstacles.

The Contextual Insight of Domain Experts

Domain experts bring a critical perspective to cross-functional teams: they ensure AI solutions align with the practical realities of their specific industry. Their insights help validate the relevance of data, the feasibility of models, and the ethical considerations of AI decisions.

For example, in a financial fraud detection project, domain experts might guide data scientists by identifying transaction patterns that signal fraudulent behavior. Their expertise ensures the model focuses on the right metrics and avoids irrelevant noise. Similarly, in healthcare, domain experts validate diagnostic models by comparing predictions with real-world patient outcomes, ensuring that the AI supports—not undermines—clinical decision-making.

Ethical oversight is another vital contribution. Domain experts often address potential societal impacts, such as ensuring models are fair and free from bias. In a credit scoring project, they might work closely with data scientists to ensure the system doesn't disproportionately disadvantage certain demographics, maintaining compliance with regulations like GDPR or Fair Lending Practices.

Achieving Synergy Through Collaboration

The strength of cross-functional teams lies in their ability to blend these diverse contributions into a cohesive effort. Each role complements the others, creating a collaborative environment where challenges are addressed holistically.

Take the example of predictive maintenance for industrial equipment. Data scientists might develop algorithms to predict when machinery is likely to fail, using sensor data to train their models. Engineers then create real-time processing systems that analyze this data and trigger alerts when issues are detected. Domain experts validate the predictions, ensuring they align with practical maintenance schedules and operational requirements. The result is a system that not only identifies potential failures but does so in a way that fits seamlessly into existing workflows.

Addressing the Challenges of Collaboration

While cross-functional teams unlock immense value, they also face unique challenges. Communication gaps, for instance, are a common issue. Specialists from different disciplines often use terminology that others may not understand. A data scientist might talk about "gradient descent optimization," while a domain expert focuses on operational KPIs. Miscommunication can lead to delays or misaligned expectations.

Clear and open communication is key to overcoming these barriers. Regular sync-ups, shared documentation platforms, and visual tools like Kanban boards or dashboards help create transparency. In a healthcare AI project, for example, weekly meetings between doctors, engineers, and data scientists can ensure that everyone stays aligned on priorities and progress.

Another common challenge is diverging priorities. Engineers might prioritize system scalability, while domain experts emphasize usability. Without alignment, these differences can create friction. Defining shared goals from the outset—balancing technical performance with business outcomes—ensures the team remains focused on the same objectives.

Finally, role clarity is essential. Ambiguity about responsibilities can lead to duplication of effort or gaps in accountability. By clearly defining roles—data scientists handle feature engineering and model development, engineers focus on deployment and integration, and domain experts validate the solution—teams can work more effectively.

Unlocking the Potential of Cross-Functional Teams

Cross-functional collaboration is more than just a way to organize work—it's the driving force behind successful AI projects. By bringing together specialists with diverse expertise, organizations can tackle challenges from every angle, creating solutions that are innovative, practical, and aligned with business needs.

The transformative power of these teams lies in their synergy. When data scientists, engineers, and domain experts work in harmony, they can create systems that go beyond technical excellence to deliver real-world impact. Whether it's a fraud detection model that integrates seamlessly into banking systems or a diagnostic tool that supports clinicians with actionable insights, cross-functional teams turn AI's potential into tangible results.

For organizations looking to harness the power of AI, investing in cross-functional collaboration isn't just a best practice—it's a competitive advantage.

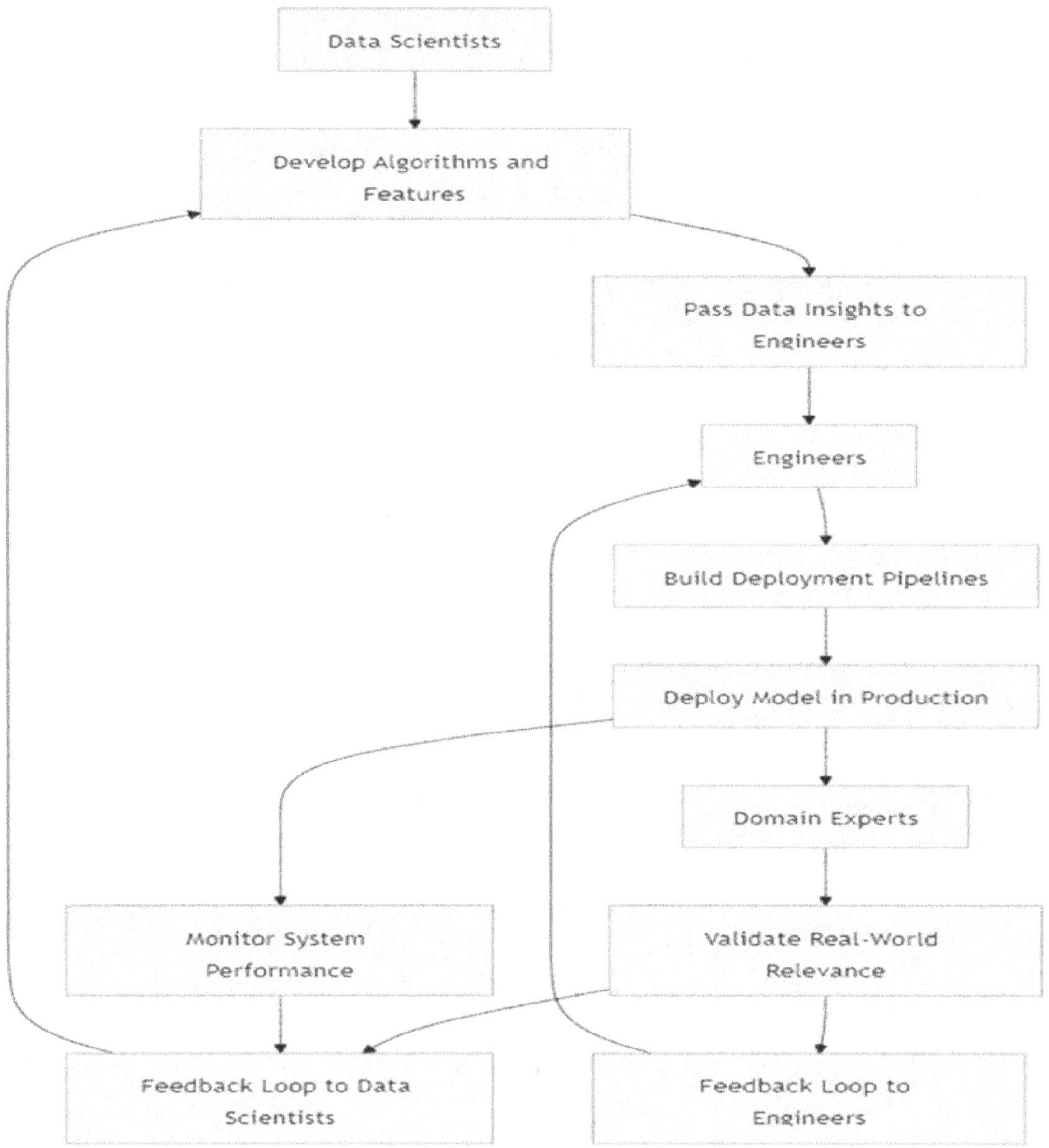

1.2.2 Skill Matrix and Requirements

Assembling a high-performing AI team requires more than just hiring talented individuals. It begins with a deep understanding of the skills needed to execute complex projects and a methodical approach to assessing, organizing, and cultivating those capabilities. A **skill matrix** is an invaluable tool in this process, providing a clear framework to evaluate the team's current strengths, identify gaps, and align resources to project demands. By systematically mapping the skills across team members and comparing them to what's required, organizations can pinpoint where upskilling or new hires are necessary, ensuring that no critical competency is overlooked.

A well-constructed skill matrix isn't just a management tool—it's a strategic advantage. It helps leaders build balanced teams, allocate resources effectively, and plan for future growth, all while fostering collaboration among team members who bring complementary strengths to the table.

The Essential Skills for AI Projects

AI projects are complex, multifaceted undertakings that draw on a multidisciplinary blend of technical, analytical, and industry-specific expertise. Broadly, these skills fall into four interconnected categories: data engineering, machine learning, domain knowledge, and cloud infrastructure proficiency. Each plays a distinct role in the lifecycle of AI development, from collecting and preparing data to deploying scalable solutions in production.

Data Engineering: Laying the Foundation Data engineering forms the backbone of AI projects. Without clean, well-structured, and accessible data, even the most advanced machine learning models will fall short of their potential. Data engineers are tasked with managing large datasets, building pipelines to move and transform data, and ensuring its quality through rigorous validation techniques.

For instance, consider a logistics AI project designed to predict shipment delays. Data engineers might build pipelines that aggregate information from multiple sources—warehouse systems, GPS trackers, and weather forecasts—before preprocessing the data to ensure consistency. Their work ensures that the machine learning models have reliable inputs, setting the stage for accurate predictions.

Machine Learning: The Core of AI Machine learning is the heart of most AI projects, driving the creation of models that can learn patterns, make predictions, or automate decision-making processes. Data scientists and machine learning engineers specialize in this domain, leveraging their knowledge of algorithms, optimization techniques, and evaluation metrics to craft solutions tailored to the project's goals.

Imagine a team developing a recommendation engine for an e-commerce platform. Data scientists experiment with techniques ranging from collaborative filtering to deep learning, iterating on models until they find one that strikes the right balance between accuracy and speed. Beyond building the model, they must fine-tune its parameters, evaluate its performance against benchmarks, and ensure it meets the project's objectives.

Domain Knowledge: Bridging AI and Real-World Applications While technical expertise is vital, domain knowledge is what makes AI solutions truly relevant. Domain experts bring a deep understanding of the industry or problem space, ensuring that models are not only accurate but also practical and aligned with the nuances of the field.

In healthcare, for example, domain experts might collaborate with data scientists to develop diagnostic tools that identify rare diseases. Their insights ensure the AI system adheres to strict regulatory standards like HIPAA, while also making sure its predictions are clinically meaningful. Without their guidance, even a technically perfect model might fail to gain traction due to gaps in its real-world applicability.

Cloud Infrastructure: Enabling Scalability As AI systems move from prototypes to production, cloud infrastructure becomes critical. Engineers with expertise in platforms like AWS, Azure, or Google Cloud ensure that these systems are scalable, secure, and efficient. They design the pipelines that deploy models, manage distributed systems, and oversee performance under real-world workloads.

Take a computer vision model used for quality control in manufacturing. Cloud engineers might set up an edge computing pipeline where the model processes images locally on factory equipment, reducing latency, while results are sent to a cloud dashboard for real-time monitoring. Their work ensures the system can handle the demands of a high-volume production environment without compromising performance.

Constructing and Using a Skill Matrix

A skill matrix brings structure to the process of team building and resource allocation. At its core, it's a grid that maps essential skills along one axis and team members along the other. Each cell in the grid reflects an individual's proficiency in a given area, whether they're a novice, proficient, or an expert. This simple yet powerful framework provides a clear view of the team's capabilities, enabling project managers to make informed decisions about task assignments, training priorities, and recruitment needs.

For example, in a skill matrix for an AI-driven marketing project, you might see that one team member excels at building ML pipelines but lacks experience with natural language processing, while another has deep expertise in NLP but limited knowledge of deployment tools. By identifying these gaps, the organization can strategically assign tasks or provide targeted training to ensure the team can tackle every phase of the project.

The skill matrix also helps teams stay agile as projects evolve. Perhaps a new requirement arises mid-project that demands expertise in reinforcement learning—a skill no current team member has mastered. With the matrix as a reference, leaders can quickly determine whether to invest in upskilling the existing team or hire a specialist to fill the gap.

Skill Matrix Example

Skill/Team Member	Data Scientist A	Engineer B	Domain Expert C	ML Engineer D
Data Preprocessing	Expert	Intermediate	Novice	Intermediate
NLP Model Development	Expert	Novice	Novice	Intermediate
Cloud Deployment	Intermediate	Expert	Novice	Expert
Domain Knowledge (Retail)	Intermediate	Novice	Expert	Novice

Turning Skills into Strategic Advantage

AI projects succeed or fail based on the collective capabilities of the team behind them. A skill matrix doesn't just highlight what a team can do today—it's a roadmap for growth, a guide to effective collaboration, and a safeguard against blind spots that could derail progress. By thoughtfully assessing and aligning skills, organizations can build teams that are not only capable but also resilient and ready to tackle the challenges of AI development.

Ultimately, the value of a skill matrix goes beyond the grid itself. It fosters a culture of intentionality, where every team member knows their strengths, understands their role, and contributes to a shared vision of success. For organizations striving to deliver cutting-edge AI solutions, this clarity and cohesion are not just helpful—they're essential.

Applying the Skill Matrix in Real Projects

Imagine a team tasked with developing an AI-powered chatbot for customer service. At the outset, they use a skill matrix to map their current capabilities against the project's requirements. The assessment reveals several key insights. The team is strong in areas like natural language processing (NLP) and data preprocessing—critical for understanding and structuring customer interactions. Deployment and backend integration skills are adequately covered but could benefit from further refinement. However, a significant gap emerges in conversational design, the specialized skillset needed to create engaging and intuitive chatbot interactions.

Armed with this knowledge, the team can take proactive steps to address the gap. They might decide to hire a user experience (UX) designer with expertise in conversational AI to ensure the chatbot's responses feel natural and align with customer expectations. Alternatively, they could invest in training an existing team member, equipping them with knowledge of frameworks like Rasa or Dialogflow. If time is of the essence, they might even bring in an external consultant to guide the design phase.

This structured approach ensures that no aspect of the project is overlooked and that the team is equipped to meet the project's objectives efficiently. By addressing gaps early, the team avoids bottlenecks later in the development process and ensures the final chatbot delivers both functionality and an exceptional user experience.

Balancing Generalists and Specialists in AI Teams

A key consideration in building an AI team is finding the right mix of generalists and specialists. While specialists bring deep expertise in areas like NLP, computer vision, or cloud infrastructure, generalists provide the flexibility to tackle diverse challenges and bridge gaps between disciplines. Together, they form a balanced team capable of addressing both the depth and breadth of skills needed for complex projects.

One effective approach to achieving this balance is to assemble a team of T-shaped professionals. These are individuals with deep expertise in a particular area, represented by the vertical stroke of the "T," and a broad understanding of related disciplines, reflected in the horizontal stroke. This combination allows team members to excel in their specialties while collaborating effectively across other domains.

Take, for example, a data scientist whose deep expertise lies in NLP. If this person also has a working knowledge of data pipeline architecture, they can seamlessly collaborate with data engineers, ensuring that their models integrate smoothly with the underlying infrastructure. Similarly, an ML engineer with basic domain knowledge—such as an understanding of healthcare workflows—can design deployment strategies that align more closely with real-world constraints, avoiding potential missteps.

This balance is particularly valuable in AI projects, where workflows are interconnected, and success depends on effective collaboration. A specialist can dive deep into solving a challenging problem, while a generalist can provide the context or cross-disciplinary insight needed to make that solution work within the broader system.

Why the Right Mix Matters

The interplay between generalists and specialists ensures that AI teams remain agile and adaptable. Specialists provide the technical depth needed to tackle complex problems, pushing the boundaries of innovation. Generalists, meanwhile, act as connectors, ensuring the team functions as a cohesive unit and that solutions address real-world requirements.

In the case of the customer service chatbot, a specialist in conversational AI might excel at creating the underlying algorithms that make the bot's responses feel human-like. However, without input from a generalist who understands the nuances of backend integration or deployment scalability, the chatbot might perform well in testing but falter when faced with real-world demands, such as handling spikes in user traffic.

By fostering a culture where both specialists and generalists thrive, organizations can create teams that are not only technically capable but also strategically aligned. These teams can navigate the complexities of AI development with confidence, delivering solutions that are both innovative and practical.

Ultimately, the mix of generalists and specialists, guided by a clear understanding of team capabilities through tools like a skill matrix, ensures that every AI project is built on a foundation of collaboration, expertise, and adaptability.

The following diagram illustrates how a skill matrix identifies gaps and aligns resources:

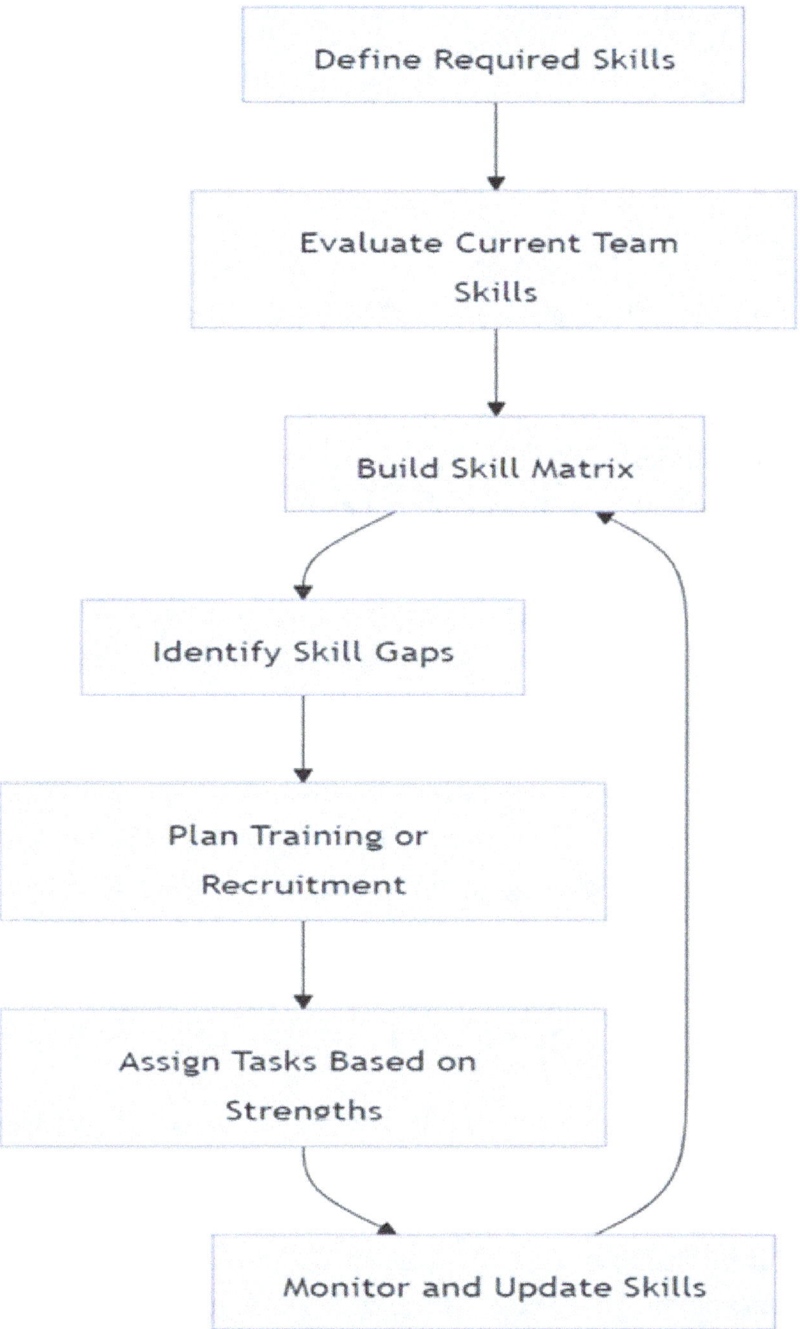

A skill matrix is an essential tool for building and managing high-performing AI teams. By systematically assessing existing capabilities, identifying gaps, and aligning skills with project objectives, organizations can ensure their teams are prepared to tackle the complexities of AI development. The inclusion of T-shaped professionals enhances collaboration and flexibility, enabling teams to adapt to evolving project requirements. Regular updates to the skill matrix ensure that the team's capabilities remain aligned with organizational goals and technological advancements, positioning the organization for sustained success in the rapidly evolving AI landscape.

1.2.3 Communication & Collaboration Patterns

AI projects thrive on collaboration, drawing expertise from diverse fields such as data science, machine learning, domain-specific knowledge, and project management. While this diversity is a strength, it can also be a source of challenges. Without clear communication frameworks, misunderstandings can arise, leading to inefficiencies and delays that slow down progress. Effective communication isn't just a nice-to-have in AI projects—it's essential to aligning goals, sharing knowledge, and ensuring that everyone is working toward the same objectives.

Centralized Communication Platforms: A Unified Space for Collaboration

One of the most effective ways to streamline communication is by using centralized platforms like Slack, Microsoft Teams, or Confluence. These tools provide a shared space where teams can discuss ideas, share updates, and store critical project documentation. By consolidating all communication and resources in one place, teams reduce the risk of information getting lost in fragmented channels like email threads or isolated conversations.

Imagine a team working on an AI-driven customer support chatbot. They might create dedicated channels within Slack for specific topics: one for discussing model updates, another for tackling data preprocessing challenges, and a third for deployment strategies. These focused discussions ensure that team members can easily access relevant information without wading through unrelated messages. Meanwhile, a tool like Confluence serves as a repository for documentation, such as workflows, model evaluation reports, or versioning logs. A well-maintained Confluence page might, for example, track the evolution of the chatbot's models, detailing performance metrics and key decisions made at each stage.

Centralizing communication fosters transparency and accessibility. Team members can quickly revisit previous discussions or access the latest updates, reducing redundant conversations and enabling faster decision-making. It's the difference between everyone being on the same page and critical details slipping through the cracks.

The Value of Regular Sync-Ups

While centralized platforms create a foundation for collaboration, regular sync-ups are equally important for maintaining alignment and momentum. These meetings give team members a chance to share progress, address dependencies, and resolve bottlenecks in real-time.

The structure and frequency of these meetings depend on the project's needs. Daily standups, for instance, are short, focused check-ins where team members share what they're working on and flag any blockers. A data scientist might mention that a feature engineering task is delayed due to inconsistencies in the dataset, prompting the data engineering team to prioritize cleaning the affected data. These quick updates keep everyone informed and help the team adapt to changes swiftly.

Weekly strategy meetings take a broader view, providing space for cross-functional discussions about milestones, priorities, and challenges. Imagine an AI project where engineers are struggling with deployment latency. In the weekly meeting, they might highlight this issue, prompting discussions about model adjustments or infrastructure upgrades. These sessions ensure that technical and business priorities remain aligned.

Finally, retrospectives at the end of each sprint offer a chance to reflect. Teams evaluate what went well, identify areas for improvement, and refine their processes for the next cycle. For example, a retrospective might reveal that unclear preprocessing requirements caused delays in model training, leading the team to improve their documentation practices going forward.

These regular sync-ups foster accountability and encourage proactive problem-solving, keeping the entire team aligned and focused on achieving project goals.

Visualization: Bringing Clarity to Progress

In AI projects, where workflows are often complex and interdependent, visualization tools like Jira, Trello, or Asana play a crucial role. These tools help teams track tasks, manage dependencies, and identify potential delays before they escalate.

Kanban boards, for instance, provide a clear snapshot of task statuses, with columns like "To Do," "In Progress," and "Done." A team might use a Jira board to track tasks such as "Clean Dataset A," "Train Model X," or "Deploy API." Each task is assigned to a specific team member, ensuring clarity about responsibilities. Meanwhile, Gantt charts offer a longer-term view, mapping out timelines and dependencies. In a project involving demand forecasting for retail, a Gantt chart might illustrate that data preprocessing must be completed before model training can begin, helping the team prioritize accordingly.

These visual tools don't just keep everyone organized—they also enhance collaboration by making dependencies explicit. For instance, if a "Data Cleaning" task is blocked, it might alert the team to reallocate resources or consider alternative datasets before the delay affects subsequent tasks. Visualization turns abstract workflows into tangible plans, keeping the team focused and on track.

Cultivating a Culture of Open Collaboration

Open collaboration is the lifeblood of successful AI teams. It's about creating an environment where team members feel comfortable sharing feedback, raising concerns, and contributing their insights without hesitation. When collaboration is truly open, teams can identify challenges early and innovate more effectively.

Encouraging feedback is a key part of this culture. For example, an engineer might point out that a model's predictions are difficult to integrate into the production system. Instead of seeing this as a roadblock, the team can view it as an opportunity to refine the model's output format, ensuring smoother deployment.

Knowledge sharing is another essential practice. Cross-functional workshops give team members a chance to learn from each other's expertise. A data scientist might lead a session on model interpretability techniques, helping domain experts understand how predictions are generated. This shared understanding not only builds trust but also improves the quality of decisions made throughout the project.

Finally, practices like pair programming or shadowing can deepen cross-functional collaboration. An ML engineer shadowing a data scientist during feature engineering, for instance, might gain valuable insights into the preprocessing requirements for future models. These experiences foster mutual understanding and break down barriers between roles, making the team stronger as a whole.

Bringing It All Together: An Example in Practice

Consider a team developing an AI-driven inventory management system. To ensure effective collaboration, they rely on a structured approach. They use Slack for quick updates and Confluence for detailed documentation, creating a centralized hub for all project-related communication. Weekly meetings provide a platform for data scientists to share model updates, engineers to discuss integration challenges, and domain experts to validate predictions against operational needs.

Meanwhile, a shared Jira board tracks tasks like "Ingest Historical Sales Data" and "Train Demand Forecasting Model." By visualizing progress and dependencies, the team ensures that everyone knows their responsibilities and timelines.

This structured communication framework not only minimizes miscommunication but also fosters collaboration across disciplines. The result is a team that works in harmony, delivering an AI solution that is both innovative and aligned with real-world needs.

The Foundation of Success

In AI projects, success hinges on effective collaboration. By establishing clear communication frameworks, fostering open dialogue, and leveraging tools that visualize progress, teams can overcome the complexities of AI development. These practices ensure that every team member—whether a data scientist, engineer, domain expert, or project manager—has the information and support they need to contribute their best work. In the end, it's not just the technology that drives successful AI projects; it's the people and the way they collaborate to bring their collective vision to life.

The following diagram illustrates the key elements of effective communication and collaboration in an AI project:

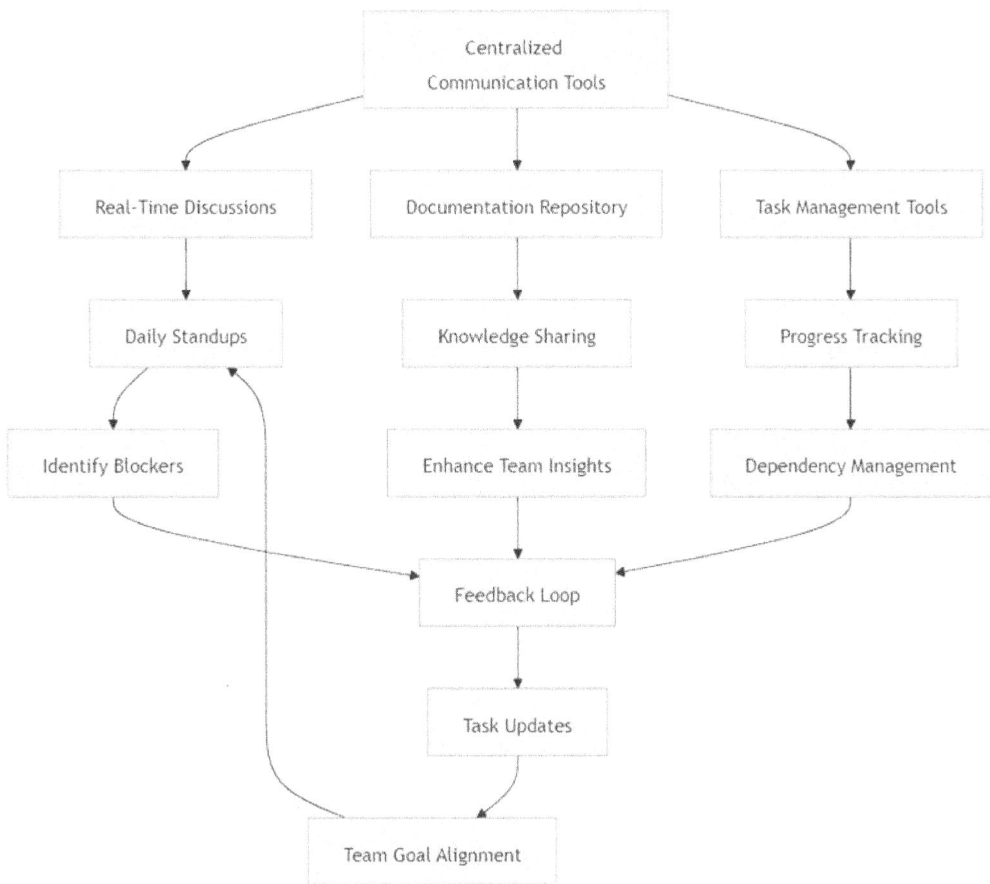

Effective communication and collaboration patterns are essential for the success of AI projects. Centralized platforms ensure seamless information sharing, regular sync-ups align goals, and visualization tools keep teams organized. By fostering open collaboration, organizations can create a culture where innovation thrives, challenges are addressed early, and AI solutions are developed efficiently and effectively. This structured approach to communication helps teams navigate the complexities of AI development, ensuring that diverse expertise is leveraged to its fullest potential.

1.3 Risk & Resource Management

Managing risks and resources is foundational to the success of any AI project. Unlike traditional software development, AI initiatives introduce unique complexities stemming from their reliance on vast datasets, iterative workflows, and computationally intensive processes. Effective risk management involves addressing uncertainties across technical, operational, and strategic dimensions, while resource management focuses on optimizing the use of computational, human, and financial assets. Together, these practices ensure that projects remain on track, budgets are respected, and outcomes are aligned with organizational goals.

1.3.1 AI-Specific Risk Assessment

AI projects come with a distinct set of risks, many of which arise from the experimental nature of building intelligent systems. These risks can be broadly categorized into technical, operational, and strategic challenges, each requiring tailored mitigation strategies.

Technical risks often stem from issues with the data and algorithms at the heart of AI systems. Model bias is a particularly pressing concern, where unrepresentative or skewed training data can lead to unfair or inaccurate predictions. Imagine an AI-powered hiring system that inadvertently favors one demographic over others because its training data failed to capture a diverse applicant pool. Addressing such risks requires a combination of diverse datasets, fairness audits, and continuous monitoring to identify and rectify biases in real time.

Another technical risk lies in overfitting, where models perform exceptionally well on training data but fail in real-world applications. For instance, a predictive maintenance model trained on machinery in one factory might struggle when applied to a different factory with unique equipment. Ensuring robust generalization through cross-validation and representative datasets is key to mitigating this issue. Similarly, algorithmic failures—unpredictable behaviors triggered by rare edge cases—can have serious consequences. An autonomous vehicle, for example, might misinterpret an unusual road sign, jeopardizing safety. Stress testing and robustness evaluations can help address such vulnerabilities.

On the operational side, risks are often tied to data quality and regulatory compliance. Poor-quality or incomplete data can derail workflows, as seen in healthcare projects where inconsistencies in patient records delay model training. Setting up reliable data pipelines and preprocessing frameworks can mitigate this challenge. Compliance with regulatory standards is another critical area, particularly in industries like finance and healthcare. Projects must adhere to laws such as GDPR or FDA guidelines, with non-compliance potentially resulting in legal penalties and reputational damage. Early involvement of legal and compliance experts can help teams navigate these complexities.

Strategic risks, meanwhile, center on alignment between AI initiatives and business goals. Unrealistic expectations can derail projects before they begin. For instance, stakeholders might assume a chatbot can seamlessly handle all customer queries from day one, only to be disappointed by the system's initial limitations. Clear, transparent communication about what AI can—and cannot—achieve helps set realistic expectations. Similarly, AI solutions that fail to deliver measurable value risk being labeled as failed investments. Deploying a cutting-edge recommendation engine that doesn't resonate with customer preferences is a prime example. Defining success metrics early ensures that technical efforts align with strategic objectives.

Mitigating these risks requires a proactive approach, starting with brainstorming sessions to identify potential challenges. Risk matrices can be used to assess the likelihood and impact of each risk, allowing teams to prioritize their efforts. Continuous monitoring is essential, with automated tools tracking potential issues like model drift or performance declines. Regular audits further ensure compliance with ethical standards, data privacy laws, and performance benchmarks.

For example, a financial institution deploying an AI-powered loan approval system might identify the risk of bias against certain demographics. To address this, the team could conduct fairness audits, retrain the model using balanced datasets, and implement a real-time bias detection tool to monitor outputs. This comprehensive approach ensures the system remains fair, accurate, and compliant.

1.3.2 Resource Allocation for Training & Infrastructure

AI projects are resource-intensive, often demanding significant computational power, specialized talent, and robust data pipelines. Efficiently managing these resources is critical for optimizing costs, maintaining timelines, and ensuring project sustainability.

Computational resources play a central role, particularly during model training. Deep learning models, for example, require substantial hardware capabilities, such as GPUs or TPUs, which are optimized for parallel computations. Training a computer vision model like ResNet-50, for instance, might take days on a single GPU but only hours on a multi-GPU setup. Cloud platforms such as AWS, Azure, and Google Cloud provide scalable solutions, enabling teams to access on-demand computational power. However, these platforms require vigilant monitoring to prevent cost overruns, especially during prolonged training cycles.

Data resources are equally critical. Acquiring high-quality datasets can involve sourcing proprietary data, integrating IoT devices, or purchasing third-party datasets. A smart city project, for example, might aggregate traffic data from both public and private sources. Once collected, raw data must be cleaned, transformed, and augmented—a process that can be streamlined with automated tools like Apache Airflow or handled by dedicated data engineers.

Human resources, meanwhile, form the backbone of any AI project. Recruiting skilled data scientists, engineers, and domain experts can be both challenging and costly, given the competitive market for AI talent. Upskilling existing team members through certifications in advanced AI frameworks or cloud platforms can be a cost-effective alternative. Providing ongoing training ensures that teams remain equipped to handle evolving challenges, from adopting new tools to addressing emerging ethical concerns.

Strategies for optimizing resources include leveraging pre-trained models, such as BERT for natural language processing tasks, which can significantly reduce training time and computational costs. Cost-effective cloud options, like spot instances or preemptible VMs, can also help manage expenses for non-critical tasks. Automating repetitive processes, such as data preprocessing, frees up valuable human resources for higher-value activities.

Consider a retail company developing a recommendation engine. By using pre-trained models for implementation and cloud GPUs for training, the team was able to reduce costs while accelerating the project timeline.

1.3.3 Budget Planning for AI Projects

Budgeting for AI projects is particularly challenging due to their exploratory nature and iterative workflows. A robust budget plan must account for both predictable expenses, such as hardware and data acquisition, and unforeseen costs that arise during experimentation.

Key budget categories typically include data, infrastructure, and talent. Data-related costs often represent a significant portion of the budget, especially in projects requiring annotated datasets. For example, annotating medical images for a diagnostic tool might involve hiring domain experts, driving up costs. Infrastructure expenses, such as hardware investments and recurring cloud fees, are another major consideration. Monitoring cloud usage closely is critical to prevent overages. Talent costs, including recruitment and training, also factor heavily into the overall budget.

Given the inherent uncertainty of AI projects, phased budgeting can be an effective strategy. Allocating funds in stages tied to specific milestones—such as data collection, model experimentation, and deployment—provides flexibility and reduces the risk of overspending. Setting aside contingency funds, typically 10–20% of the total budget, ensures the team can address unexpected challenges, such as acquiring additional data or upgrading infrastructure.

It's also important to account for post-deployment costs, as AI systems require ongoing monitoring, retraining, and updates to remain effective. For example, a logistics company developing an AI-powered route optimization tool might allocate $500,000 to the project, dividing it into $200,000 for data collection and preprocessing, $150,000 for model development, $100,000 for cloud resources, and $50,000 for post-deployment maintenance.

This structured approach to budgeting ensures that resources are used efficiently and that the project is equipped to handle both anticipated and unforeseen demands, paving the way for long-term success.

The Road to Sustainable AI Development

Effective risk and resource management are not just supportive practices in AI projects—they are fundamental to their success. By proactively identifying risks, optimizing resource allocation, and planning budgets with foresight, teams can navigate the complexities of AI development with confidence. This holistic approach ensures that projects deliver on their promises, driving innovation while staying aligned with organizational goals.

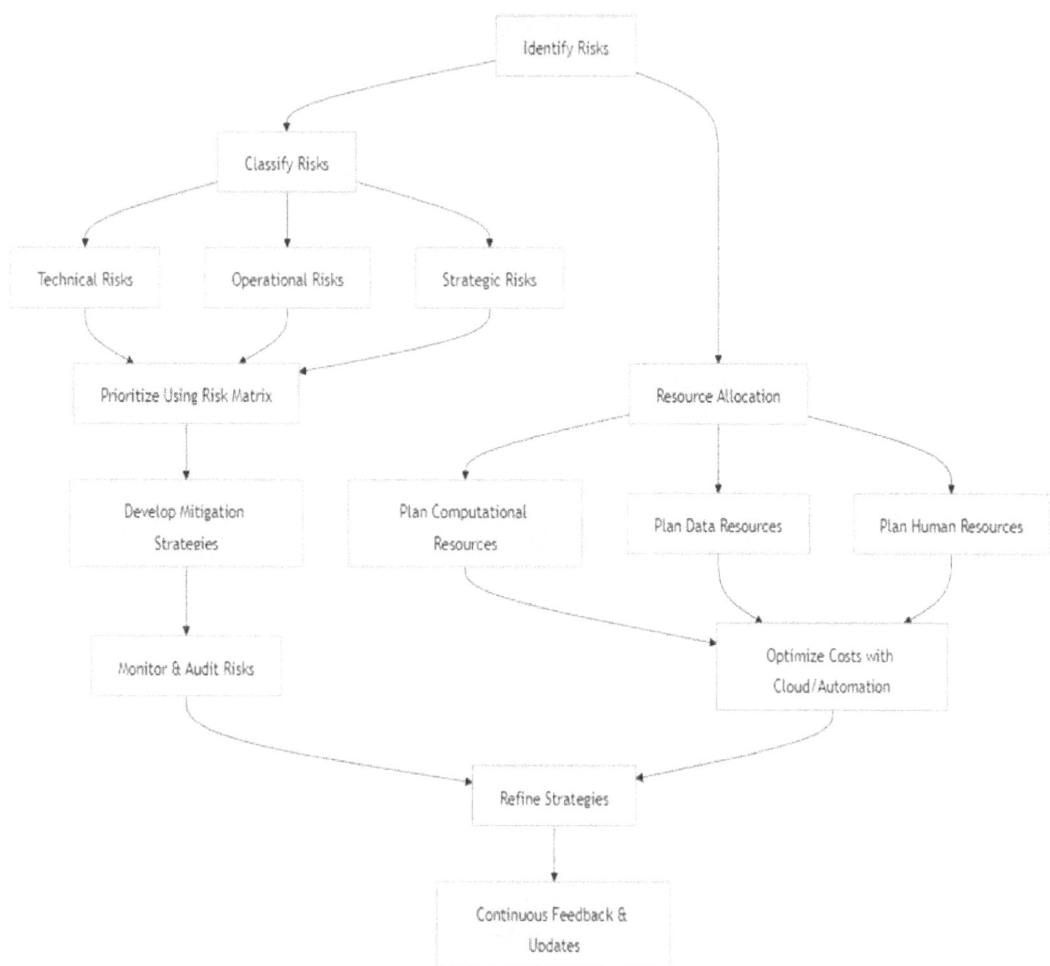

Managing risks and resources effectively ensures that AI projects remain on track, scalable, and aligned with business objectives. By addressing technical, operational, and strategic risks early, optimizing resources, and planning budgets with flexibility, organizations can navigate the complexities of AI development while minimizing disruptions. Proactive strategies and continuous monitoring provide a foundation for long-term success.

1.4 Stakeholder Management

The collaborative nature of AI projects makes stakeholder management an essential part of ensuring success. These initiatives often bring together diverse groups, including business executives, domain experts, end-users, and regulatory bodies, each with their own priorities and expectations. Unlike traditional software projects, AI development involves a high degree of experimentation and uncertainty, requiring careful communication and alignment throughout the project lifecycle. Managing stakeholders effectively not only keeps projects on track but also ensures they deliver measurable outcomes aligned with organizational goals.

To achieve this, teams must focus on three key areas of stakeholder management: setting realistic expectations, reporting progress in meaningful ways, and managing changes with transparency and precision.

1.4.1 Expectation Setting in AI Projects

One of the most challenging aspects of managing stakeholders in AI projects is helping them understand what AI can and cannot achieve. AI often carries a promise of transformative impact, but the path to realizing that impact is iterative, requiring continuous refinement and adaptation. Setting realistic expectations from the start can help prevent disappointment, foster collaboration, and build trust.

Stakeholders may come to the table with overly ambitious assumptions about AI's capabilities. For example, they might envision a customer service chatbot that can handle all complex queries seamlessly from day one. While the potential is exciting, the reality is that technical limitations, particularly in natural language processing, often mean such systems start by handling simpler tasks before evolving into more sophisticated tools. Misaligned goals can also present challenges; a technical team might prioritize metrics like accuracy or precision, while business stakeholders are more focused on customer satisfaction or cost savings.

To manage these challenges, teams need to approach expectation setting with a combination of education and transparency. Stakeholders should understand the iterative nature of AI development, where initial results might fall short of ultimate goals but lay the groundwork for future improvements. It's also important to establish clear, measurable objectives that balance technical performance with business outcomes. For instance, rather than a vague goal like "reducing churn," the team might work toward "predicting 75% of high-risk customers with 80% accuracy."

Take the example of a legal AI project aimed at automating document review. Initially, stakeholders might expect full automation, imagining a system that can instantly handle all legal paperwork without error. By explaining that the system will begin by assisting with repetitive, lower-stakes tasks—such as flagging standard clauses for review—before progressing to more complex analyses, the project team can set realistic expectations. This transparency not only builds trust but also secures long-term support as the system evolves.

1.4.2 Progress Reporting & Metrics

Keeping stakeholders engaged and aligned requires regular updates that reflect both achievements and challenges. However, progress reporting in AI projects differs from traditional software reporting. AI's iterative nature means that updates often include nuanced metrics and evolving outcomes, which need to be communicated clearly to diverse audiences.

Transparency is critical in progress reporting. Regular updates help stakeholders understand how the project is evolving, where challenges lie, and how these challenges are being addressed. They also ensure alignment, allowing teams to adjust priorities based on new insights or shifting business needs.

Highlighting incremental successes, even small ones, maintains enthusiasm and reassures stakeholders that the project is moving in the right direction.

Effective reporting hinges on selecting the right metrics and tailoring them to the audience. For technical stakeholders, metrics like precision, recall, or F1-score provide insight into model performance. A spam detection system, for instance, might highlight an F1-score of 0.85 as a significant milestone. For business executives, however, the focus might shift to outcomes such as cost savings or customer satisfaction. Platforms like Tableau or Power BI can help teams create visual dashboards that present these metrics in an accessible way, showing real-time updates on progress like improved click-through rates for a recommendation engine.

Consider a retail company developing an AI-powered demand forecasting tool. Their progress reports might highlight three key areas: the percentage of historical sales data that has been cleaned and preprocessed (e.g., 90%), improvements in model accuracy (e.g., from 75% to 85%), and tangible business outcomes (e.g., a 15% reduction in stockouts during the pilot deployment). By framing updates in a way that resonates with different stakeholders, the team builds confidence and sustains support throughout the project.

1.4.3 Change Management Strategies

AI projects are inherently dynamic. New data might emerge, algorithms might need refinement, or business priorities might shift mid-development. Change is inevitable, but how it's managed can mean the difference between success and failure. Effective change management ensures that adjustments are handled smoothly without losing stakeholder alignment or project momentum.

Resistance to change is a common hurdle. Stakeholders may worry that changes will increase costs, extend timelines, or complicate workflows. For example, switching from a rule-based system to a machine learning model might face pushback if stakeholders fear the added complexity. Changes can also ripple across interdependent workflows, where a delay in data preprocessing impacts model training and deployment timelines.

To navigate these challenges, it's essential to establish a governance framework for evaluating and approving changes. A steering committee with representation from both technical and business stakeholders can ensure that decisions are well-informed and aligned with organizational goals. Clear communication is equally important—stakeholders need to understand why changes are necessary and how they contribute to long-term success. Breaking changes into manageable phases can further reduce disruption, allowing the team to implement adjustments incrementally while maintaining steady progress.

Consider an AI fraud detection project that encounters a critical challenge: its dataset is insufficient for detecting emerging fraud patterns. Rather than overhauling the project entirely, the team communicates the need for additional data collection and proposes a phased approach. New data is integrated gradually, allowing existing models to be refined without delaying other aspects of development. By providing a revised timeline with clear milestones, the team maintains transparency and ensures continued stakeholder trust.

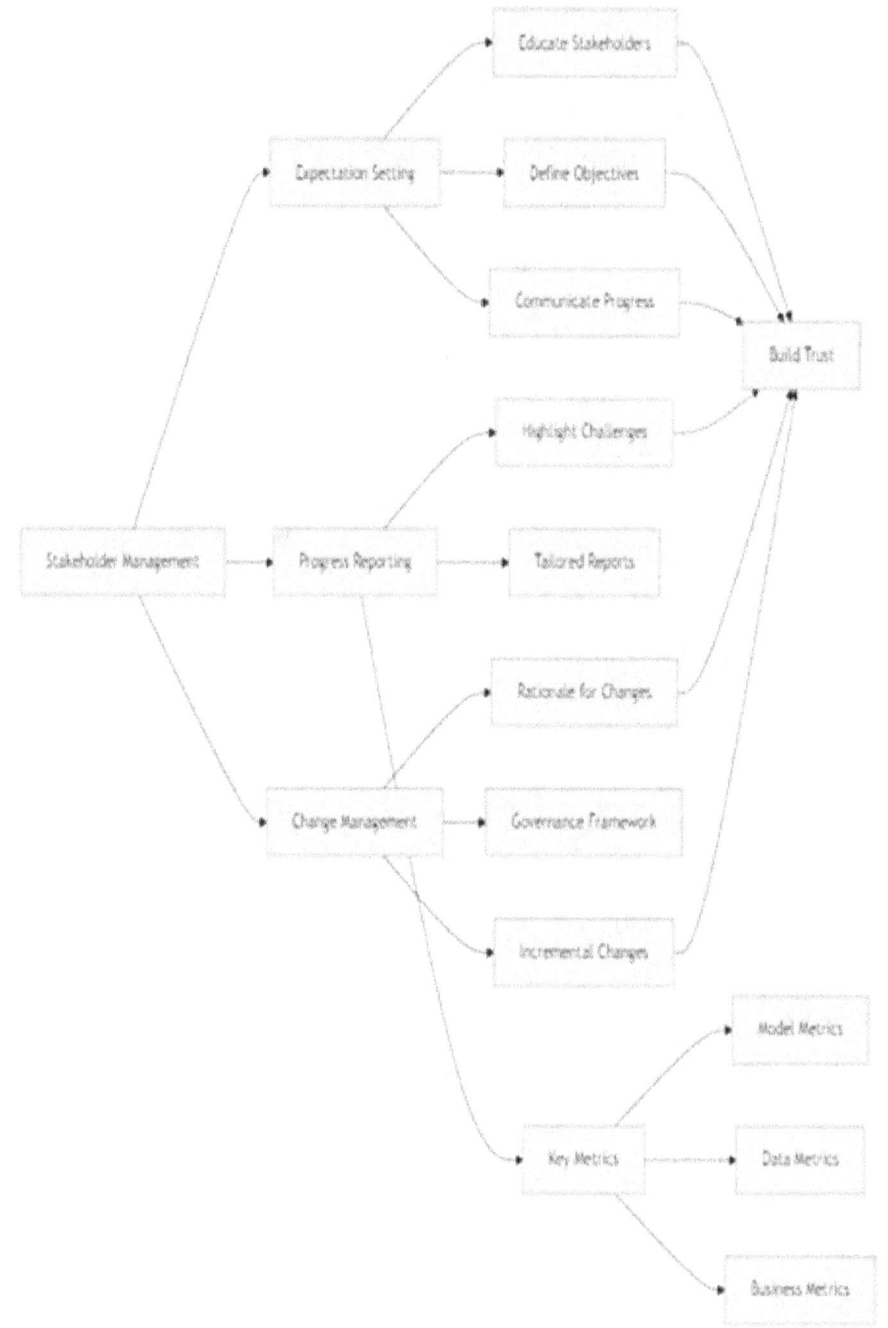

Stakeholder management is critical to the success of AI projects. By setting realistic expectations, reporting progress transparently, and managing changes effectively, organizations can align stakeholders with project goals and sustain their support throughout the AI lifecycle. This structured approach fosters collaboration, builds trust, and ensures that AI initiatives deliver measurable value.

Chapter 2
Testing & Quality Assurance for AI Systems

Testing and quality assurance are vital to building AI systems that perform reliably in dynamic, ever-changing environments. Unlike traditional software, AI systems are deeply intertwined with data, and their behavior can vary significantly based on the quality and nature of that data. This complexity makes comprehensive testing essential, starting with the most granular level: unit testing.

Unit testing is the foundation of QA practices. It focuses on verifying the correctness of individual components in isolation, ensuring they work as expected before being integrated into the larger system. In the context of AI, these components can range from data preprocessing scripts and feature engineering modules to individual machine learning algorithms. Testing these pieces rigorously lays the groundwork for a robust, high-performing AI system.

2.1.1 Unit Testing ML Components

At its core, unit testing in AI systems involves validating whether each standalone function, module, or script behaves as intended. Take data preprocessing as an example. A script tasked with normalizing numerical features should handle edge cases like missing values or extreme outliers without breaking. If this script fails, it can cascade issues downstream, rendering the entire model unreliable. By catching these errors early, unit testing helps prevent costly troubleshooting later in the development cycle.

Feature engineering, another critical aspect, also benefits from unit testing. Imagine a function designed to calculate moving averages over a sliding window of data points. If this function produces inaccurate results for certain window sizes, the model it feeds will likely fail to capture important patterns in the data. A unit test ensures that the feature is computed correctly under various conditions, safeguarding the integrity of the data pipeline.

Algorithm testing, meanwhile, focuses on verifying the behavior of machine learning models in controlled scenarios. For instance, a K-Means clustering algorithm should consistently produce the same clusters when given the same data and parameters. If it doesn't, there could be an implementation issue or a random seed problem that needs fixing before the model goes live.

Boundary testing is also indispensable. AI systems often encounter edge cases in real-world applications, and unit testing helps ensure these scenarios are handled gracefully. A regression model, for instance, should return sensible outputs—or at the very least, avoid crashing—when given zero or null inputs.

Finally, mocking plays a significant role in isolating dependencies during unit testing. By simulating external systems, such as databases or APIs, mocking allows developers to test specific components in isolation without introducing unnecessary complexity. For example, a mock database can supply predefined datasets to test how a preprocessing script handles specific data quirks.

Benefits of Unit Testing

The benefits of unit testing extend far beyond error detection. By isolating and validating individual components, it reduces debugging complexity, making it easier to pinpoint issues when they arise. It also ensures that code remains maintainable—developers can make changes confidently, knowing that existing functionality is safeguarded by tests.

Unit testing fosters reproducibility, a cornerstone of good AI practices. When tested components yield consistent results under controlled inputs, it becomes easier to debug and refine the system. For instance, a predictive maintenance function that detects temperature anomalies in industrial sensor data can be tested to ensure it flags values outside a specific range (say, 60–80°C). Once this function is verified, developers can build on it without worrying about its reliability.

Implementing Unit Testing in AI Projects

The workflow for unit testing in AI projects is both methodical and iterative. It begins by identifying the key components that require testing. These might include data preprocessing scripts, feature engineering modules, and machine learning algorithms. Once these components are identified, developers write test cases for each, simulating real-world scenarios using synthetic data or mocked inputs.

Automation is a critical part of the process. By integrating unit tests into continuous integration/continuous deployment (CI/CD) pipelines, teams ensure that tests are run automatically every time new code is committed. This not only streamlines quality assurance but also creates a culture of accountability, where every developer contributes to maintaining system reliability.

For example, consider a predictive maintenance system for industrial machinery. One of its components might be a function designed to detect temperature anomalies in sensor data. A well-written unit test would simulate various scenarios, such as normal temperature ranges, sudden spikes, and missing values, to ensure the function behaves as expected. If the function incorrectly flags normal readings or fails to identify extreme ones, the test results will highlight the problem, allowing developers to address it before deployment.

Tools for Unit Testing AI Systems

Several tools make unit testing efficient and effective, particularly in AI projects. Pytest is a popular choice among Python developers due to its flexibility and extensive plugin support. It's particularly useful for writing tests for data preprocessing scripts, where edge cases often emerge. For developers who prefer a more structured approach, Python's built-in unittest library offers a straightforward way to create organized test suites. Mocking tools, such as unittest.mock or pytest-mock, enable the isolation of dependencies, allowing teams to focus on testing specific components without interference from external systems.

By leveraging these tools, teams can establish a robust unit testing framework that not only ensures quality but also accelerates development by catching issues early and reducing rework.

Unit Testing Workflow

To illustrate the impact of unit testing, consider a real-world example. A team working on a predictive maintenance system for industrial machinery needed to build a function that detects temperature anomalies. The function was critical—it would flag abnormal sensor readings, potentially preventing equipment failures.

Through unit testing, the team simulated various scenarios: normal readings, extreme spikes, and missing data points. One test revealed that the function incorrectly flagged borderline temperatures as anomalies, which could lead to unnecessary maintenance alerts. By refining the function and retesting, the team ensured that it only flagged genuinely problematic readings.

This early detection of issues saved time and effort later in the project. When the function was integrated into the larger system, the team could be confident in its reliability, allowing them to focus on higher-level testing and optimization.

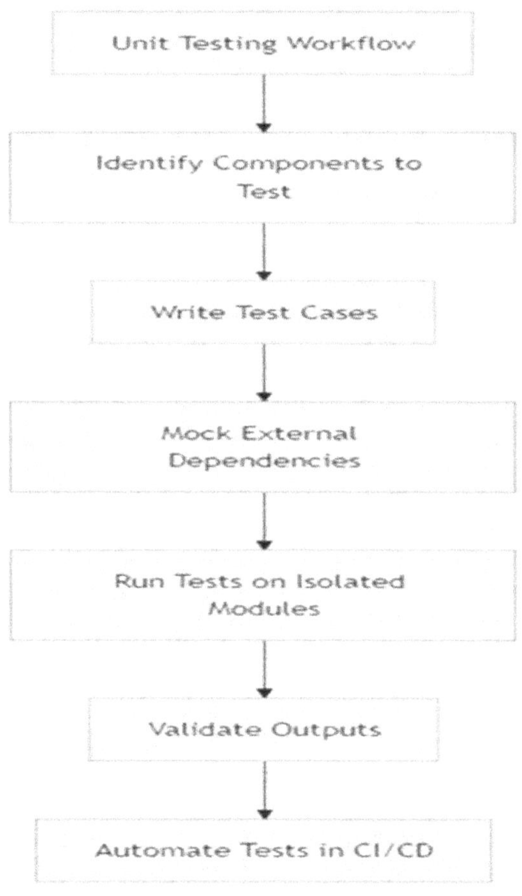

Unit Testing Workflow

Unit testing is more than a technical necessity—it's a foundation for building confidence in AI systems. By rigorously validating individual components, teams can ensure that their systems are accurate, reliable, and ready for integration. For AI projects, where data-driven processes are inherently complex, this level of assurance is invaluable.

In the end, unit testing isn't just about catching errors; it's about creating a development environment where innovation can flourish without sacrificing quality. With the right tools, processes, and mindset, unit testing becomes a cornerstone of delivering AI solutions that meet—and exceed—stakeholder expectations.

2.1.2 Integration Testing Approaches

Integration testing is a critical step in ensuring that the components of an AI system work seamlessly together. While unit testing focuses on verifying individual modules in isolation, integration testing evaluates how these components interact. This is particularly important in AI projects, where data pipelines, machine learning models, APIs, and user interfaces are deeply interconnected. The goal is not just to verify that each part functions correctly but to ensure that the entire system operates as intended, from end to end.

For example, an AI-powered recommendation engine relies on multiple components: data pipelines that preprocess user preferences, models that generate predictions, and APIs that deliver these recommendations to a front-end application. Integration testing ensures that data flows smoothly through each stage, that the model receives inputs in the correct format, and that the API responds with accurate results within acceptable time limits. Without thorough integration testing, these interdependencies can easily become points of failure.

The Goals of Integration Testing

At its core, integration testing ensures that the combined components of an AI system can exchange data, execute workflows, and achieve their objectives reliably. This involves several key objectives, starting with validating data flow. AI systems are data-driven, and any misstep in the flow—from ingestion to preprocessing, training, and inference—can compromise the entire system. Imagine a scenario where raw data from IoT sensors must be cleaned and transformed before being fed into a training pipeline. Integration testing verifies that these steps occur seamlessly and that no critical transformations are skipped or misapplied.

Another goal is to validate the inputs and outputs of machine learning models. A classification model served via an API, for instance, must receive inputs in the correct format and return outputs—such as class labels or probabilities—that align with expectations. Even a minor mismatch, such as an unexpected null value in the input, can cause errors or inconsistencies.

Integration testing also detects interoperability issues, such as mismatches in data formats or parameter expectations between components. Testing APIs, for example, might reveal that an endpoint fails to handle invalid payloads gracefully, leading to unexpected crashes. Finally, integration testing helps simulate real-world interactions, exposing latent bugs that might only arise under certain conditions. For instance, an AI chatbot might perform well in a single language but struggle when interacting with users across multiple regions or languages.

Real-World Integration Testing Scenarios

Integration testing scenarios in AI projects are as varied as the systems themselves. One common scenario involves the integration of machine learning models with data pipelines. Here, testing ensures that preprocessing scripts correctly transform incoming data before it reaches the model. Consider a feature engineering module that encodes categorical variables—an integration test would verify that these encodings are consistent and error-free, enabling smooth training and inference.

Another critical area is API integration testing. For AI systems that serve models via APIs, such as recommendation engines or fraud detection tools, testing focuses on verifying that endpoints function as intended. For instance, a recommendation engine's API should process user preferences efficiently and return relevant product suggestions in under 100 milliseconds. If the API fails to handle large payloads or introduces latency, it could degrade the user experience.

Interdependent components, such as feature extraction scripts and model inference modules, also require close scrutiny. Integration tests validate that outputs from one component align with the input expectations of the next. For example, if a feature extraction script generates vectors with missing values, these issues need to be caught and resolved before the vectors are passed to the model.

Integration Testing Workflow

Effective integration testing begins with identifying the key points where components interact. These integration points might include the handoff between data ingestion pipelines and preprocessing scripts, the connection between feature engineering modules and machine learning models, or the interaction between APIs and user interfaces. Once these points are mapped out, mock or synthetic data is used to simulate real-world scenarios. For example, a set of dummy payloads might be created to test API endpoints under various conditions, including edge cases.

Automation plays a pivotal role in ensuring that integration tests are both consistent and efficient. Tools like Postman, widely used for API testing, allow teams to validate request and response behaviors systematically. Similarly, frameworks like Jenkins can automate the execution of integration tests, embedding them into continuous integration/continuous deployment (CI/CD) pipelines. This ensures that every code change is tested for potential issues, reducing the risk of introducing bugs during development.

End-to-end validation rounds out the workflow, with tests designed to simulate complete workflows from start to finish. For instance, a fraud detection system might be tested on a batch of transactions, ensuring that raw data flows through preprocessing, model inference, and alert generation without errors.

Tools for Integration Testing

Integration testing relies on a suite of tools tailored to different aspects of the workflow. Postman is invaluable for testing RESTful APIs, allowing teams to verify everything from payload handling to latency. Pytest, a versatile testing framework for Python, is ideal for validating interactions between scripts and modules. Mocking frameworks, such as unittest.mock, simulate external services to isolate specific components for testing.

The benefits of integration testing are both immediate and long-lasting. By detecting compatibility issues early, teams can avoid the costly debugging that arises when errors propagate through the system. Integration testing also enhances system reliability, ensuring that workflows are robust to edge cases and unexpected inputs. By simulating real-world scenarios, it prepares AI systems to perform consistently in production, reducing the likelihood of failures or downtime.

A Practical Example

Consider an AI-powered recommendation engine for an e-commerce platform. One critical integration point is the interaction between the feature extraction module and the recommendation API. During testing, the team simulates real-world scenarios to ensure the API receives correctly formatted feature vectors and returns valid product recommendations. Tests might involve submitting payloads of varying sizes to evaluate the API's ability to handle large requests without performance degradation. If an issue arises—such as an unexpected delay in processing or inaccurate recommendations—the integration test pinpoints the problem, allowing the team to address it before deployment.

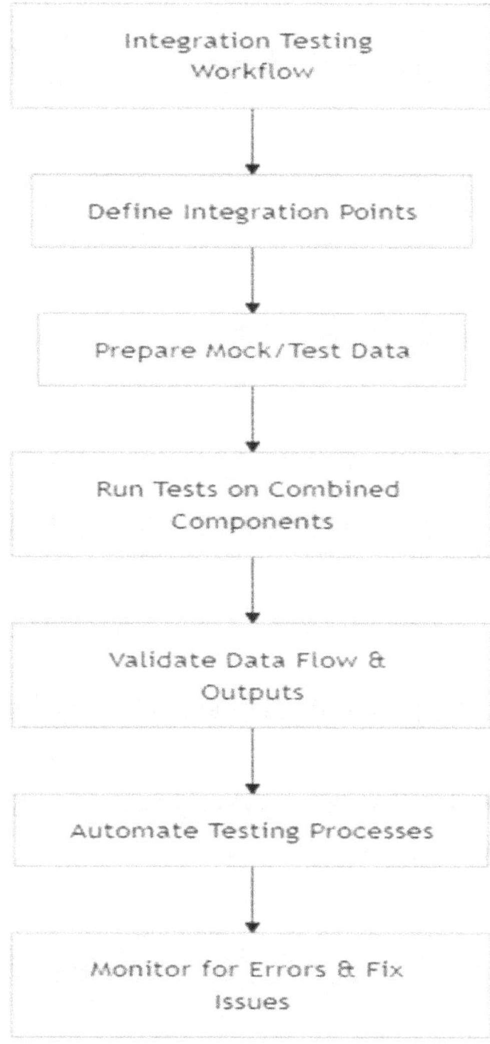

Integration Testing Workflow

Building Confidence Through Integration Testing

In AI systems, where interdependencies are the norm, integration testing provides the assurance that every component contributes to a cohesive, functional whole. By validating data flows, detecting interoperability issues, and simulating real-world interactions, integration testing bridges the gap between isolated components and end-to-end system performance.

When done well, integration testing doesn't just catch bugs—it builds confidence. It ensures that AI systems can meet the demands of their intended environments, delivering reliable results and a seamless user experience. In an era where AI solutions are becoming central to business success, robust integration testing is not just a best practice—it's a necessity.

2.1.3 End-to-End System Testing

End-to-end (E2E) system testing represents the culmination of the testing process in AI projects, ensuring that the system functions as a cohesive whole under real-world conditions. Unlike unit or integration testing, which focus on individual components or their interactions, E2E testing evaluates the entire system's behavior, from data ingestion and preprocessing to model inference and user interaction. The goal is to simulate actual workflows, uncover any bottlenecks or failures, and confirm that the system meets both functional and non-functional requirements.

For AI systems, where multiple components must work together seamlessly—data pipelines, machine learning models, APIs, and user interfaces—E2E testing is crucial. It provides confidence that the system can handle complex workflows, deliver expected outcomes, and provide a positive user experience, even under challenging or unexpected conditions.

Goals of End-to-End Testing

At its heart, E2E testing validates the overall behavior of the system, ensuring that it functions as expected when all components are integrated. Consider an AI-powered search engine. The system must correctly process user queries, send them through a preprocessing pipeline, generate results via a machine learning model, and rank these results appropriately before delivering them to the user interface. E2E testing confirms that each of these steps works together seamlessly, without disruptions or missteps.

Another critical aspect of E2E testing is simulating real-world scenarios. For example, an autonomous vehicle's AI system might be tested in a simulated urban environment, where it encounters traffic, pedestrians, and unexpected obstacles. These scenarios help uncover latent issues that may not surface in isolated or controlled testing environments.

The user experience is another vital area of focus. Whether it's ensuring that a sentiment analysis tool categorizes customer reviews accurately or that an AI chatbot responds promptly to user queries, E2E testing evaluates how the system interacts with end-users. By emphasizing UX, teams can ensure that the system is not only functional but also intuitive and reliable.

Finally, E2E testing helps identify bottlenecks and failures, such as performance lags or workflow disruptions. For instance, an AI-powered customer service chatbot might function well during normal usage but experience significant latency during peak hours. Testing under these conditions allows teams to address performance issues before they impact end-users.

Steps in End-to-End System Testing

The first step in E2E testing is defining the scope, which involves identifying the starting point, the endpoint, and all intermediate processes of the workflow. Take a predictive maintenance system, for example. The workflow might begin with IoT sensors collecting raw machine data, followed by preprocessing, anomaly detection, and finally, generating notifications for operators about potential failures. Mapping out this sequence provides a clear framework for testing.

Simulating real-world conditions is equally important. For a recommendation system, this might involve feeding the model diverse user behavior data to evaluate its performance across different customer profiles. The goal is to recreate the types of challenges the system will face in production.

Test cases should cover a range of scenarios, including typical workflows, edge cases, and stress conditions. A fraud detection system, for instance, might be tested with datasets containing legitimate transactions, clear-cut fraud cases, and ambiguous or borderline examples. Such testing ensures that the system can handle a variety of situations gracefully.

Automation is a powerful tool for E2E testing, enabling teams to validate workflows repeatedly and consistently. Tools like Apache Airflow can automate machine learning pipeline validation, ensuring that data flows correctly from ingestion to model training and deployment. Monitoring and analyzing results is the final step, where logs, performance metrics, and error reports are reviewed to identify weak points. For instance, API response times can be measured to ensure they meet latency requirements.

Key Areas of Focus

User interaction testing is central to E2E validation, as it determines how well the system handles inputs and delivers outputs. A voice assistant, for example, must accurately process voice commands across different accents and respond appropriately.

Another area of focus is workflow validation. In an AI training pipeline, raw data must pass through preprocessing, feature extraction, and model training stages, with each step producing the expected outputs for the next. E2E testing confirms that this sequence functions smoothly, catching any disruptions in the data flow.

Performance benchmarking ensures that the system can handle real-world demands. A document classification API might be stress-tested by sending a high volume of simultaneous requests, measuring its throughput, latency, and resource utilization under load. This type of testing is particularly important for systems deployed in environments with fluctuating traffic or usage patterns.

Tools for End-to-End Testing

A range of tools can facilitate E2E testing for AI systems. Selenium is widely used for automating web-based workflows, such as testing the accuracy and responsiveness of an AI-powered dashboard. Locust is another popular choice for load testing, allowing teams to simulate high traffic scenarios and evaluate system scalability. Apache Airflow excels in validating machine learning pipelines, ensuring that dependencies between components are correctly managed.

By leveraging these tools, teams can create a comprehensive testing framework that validates not only the system's functionality but also its resilience, scalability, and readiness for real-world deployment.

Example in Practice

To illustrate the importance of E2E testing, consider a demand forecasting system for a retail chain. The system ingests sales data from multiple stores, preprocesses it, and uses machine learning to generate predictions for replenishment schedules.

During E2E testing, the team might simulate daily workflows by feeding the system mock sales data. The preprocessing scripts would be validated to ensure they correctly clean and aggregate the data before passing it to the forecasting model. The model's predictions would then be evaluated for accuracy and timeliness, while the system's ability to alert stakeholders about anomalies, such as unexpected demand spikes, would also be tested.

In this example, the E2E test might reveal a critical issue: the alert system fails to detect certain anomalies during peak loads, potentially leaving stores unprepared for surges in demand. By identifying this bottleneck, the team can optimize the system's performance and ensure that it operates reliably under all conditions.

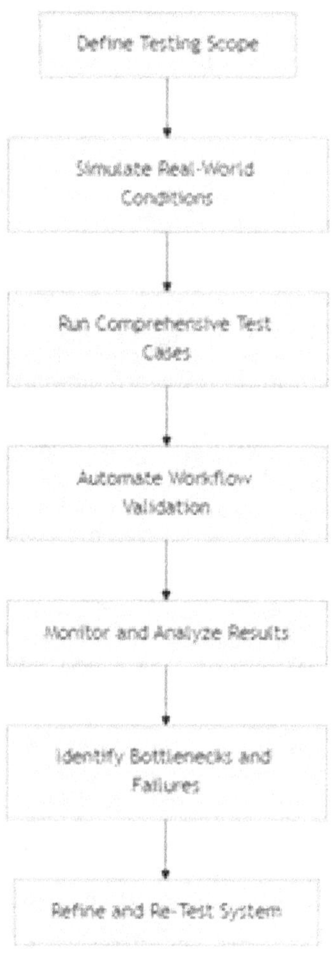

End-to-End Testing Workflow

E2E testing provides a holistic validation of AI systems, ensuring they function seamlessly as a unified whole. By simulating real-world scenarios, evaluating user experience, and identifying performance bottlenecks, E2E testing prepares AI systems for the complexities of production environments.

More than just a technical exercise, E2E testing builds confidence—for both development teams and stakeholders. It ensures that AI systems not only meet functional requirements but also deliver the reliability, scalability, and usability needed to succeed in real-world applications. In an era where AI is increasingly central to business operations, robust E2E testing is an indispensable part of delivering systems that users can trust.

2.2.1 Data Quality Validation

In the world of AI, data is not just an input—it is the foundation upon which entire systems are built. The reliability, accuracy, and fairness of a machine learning model hinge on the quality of the data it is trained on. Data quality validation plays a crucial role in ensuring that datasets meet the necessary standards to support effective training, testing, and deployment. Without rigorous validation, issues such as missing values, inconsistencies, or biases can seep into the dataset, undermining model performance and trustworthiness.

Think of data quality as the scaffolding for constructing an intricate structure. If the scaffolding is unstable or incomplete, the structure—no matter how expertly designed—will falter. AI systems, which are inherently data-driven, rely on rigorous data validation to ensure their robustness and reliability.

Key Dimensions of Data Quality

When evaluating data quality, five key dimensions often serve as benchmarks: completeness, consistency, accuracy, timeliness, and representativeness.

Completeness is about ensuring that no essential information is missing from the dataset. Imagine a sales forecasting system trying to predict demand for products, but the dataset lacks entries for certain categories. Without these, the model's predictions will be inherently flawed for those items, creating gaps in inventory planning.

Consistency focuses on ensuring that data is uniform and standardized across sources. For instance, if one data source uses the date format "YYYY-MM-DD" while another uses "MM/DD/YYYY," merging these without harmonizing the formats can lead to errors in time-series analysis.

Accuracy examines whether the data aligns with real-world facts. A healthcare AI system that misrepresents a patient's age due to incorrect entries could skew diagnostic predictions, potentially leading to serious consequences. This dimension is critical for maintaining the integrity of AI predictions.

Timeliness ensures that the data is current and relevant for the system's intended use. A real-time recommendation engine, for example, cannot rely on outdated user interaction data—it would suggest irrelevant products, frustrating users and decreasing engagement.

Finally, **representativeness** checks whether the dataset reflects the diversity of the target population. A facial recognition model trained predominantly on images of one demographic will likely perform poorly on others, perpetuating biases and inequities in its outcomes. Ensuring representativeness helps prevent such disparities and improves model fairness.

Common Data Quality Issues in AI Systems

Several common issues often emerge when preparing data for AI systems. Missing values are one of the most frequent problems, where critical fields in a dataset are left null or empty. For example, a customer churn dataset missing billing information for some users can render churn predictions incomplete or incorrect.

Outliers and anomalies present another challenge. These extreme values, such as an exceptionally high transaction amount in a financial dataset, can distort model training and make the system overly sensitive to rare but atypical cases.

Bias in data is perhaps the most insidious issue. Training data that does not accurately represent the target population can lead to skewed predictions. Consider a loan approval dataset that historically favored certain demographics over others—if left uncorrected, the model will likely replicate and perpetuate this bias.

Lastly, duplicate records can inflate the size of the dataset and skew the results. Redundant entries in a sales database, for example, might give the false impression of repeated customer purchases, impacting demand forecasting models.

Steps in Data Quality Validation

The journey to achieving high-quality data begins with data profiling, an exploratory analysis that provides insights into the dataset's structure, distribution, and potential issues. Tools like Pandas Profiling or Great Expectations can automatically generate detailed reports, highlighting areas requiring attention. This step lays the groundwork for identifying specific problems, such as missing fields or inconsistent formats.

Once the dataset has been profiled, completeness checks help ensure that no critical information is missing. For example, in a customer churn dataset, it's important to verify that all records include necessary attributes, such as contract start and end dates, to enable accurate predictions.

Next, inconsistency detection addresses discrepancies in data formats, units, or scales. A weather dataset might contain temperature readings in both Celsius and Fahrenheit, creating potential confusion. Standardizing these to a single unit ensures uniformity.

Bias detection is another critical step, using statistical methods to uncover imbalances. For example, a recommendation engine's dataset might overrepresent one demographic group, skewing predictions toward their preferences while ignoring others. Identifying and correcting this bias helps ensure fairness in outcomes.

Finally, data is validated against business rules, which are domain-specific constraints that guide logical checks. In an e-commerce context, for instance, order amounts must always be non-negative. Ensuring such rules are met helps maintain data integrity and relevance.

Tools for Data Quality Validation

Tools like **Great Expectations** and **Pandas Profiling** make data quality validation efficient and repeatable. Great Expectations, for instance, allows teams to define custom validation checks, such as ensuring that no column contains null values or that a field's values fall within specified ranges. Meanwhile, Pandas Profiling generates comprehensive summaries, quickly surfacing anomalies for further investigation.

For projects requiring streamlined workflows, tools like **DataPrep** simplify the process of cleaning and validating data in Python, reducing the time spent on manual checks.

Benefits of Data Quality Validation

The benefits of thorough data quality validation extend far beyond the immediate gains in model performance. High-quality data minimizes the risk of errors propagating through workflows, reducing operational risks. It also ensures compliance with data privacy and regulatory standards, particularly in sensitive domains like healthcare and finance.

At its core, data quality validation is about building trust. Whether it's a healthcare model diagnosing critical illnesses or a recommendation engine suggesting the perfect product, validated data ensures that AI systems operate with accuracy, reliability, and fairness. By investing in rigorous validation practices, organizations lay a solid foundation for AI systems that deliver consistent and meaningful results.

Example in Practice

Imagine a bank developing a credit scoring system to evaluate loan eligibility. The dataset includes transaction histories, income levels, and credit scores. During the validation process, missing values in income levels are detected, prompting the team to use imputation techniques to fill these gaps. Numeric features, such as credit scores, are standardized to a consistent scale to ensure uniformity across all records. A bias check reveals underrepresentation of certain demographics, prompting the team to balance the dataset to ensure fair treatment of all applicants.

The result is a cleaner, unbiased dataset that not only improves the model's accuracy but also aligns with ethical standards, ensuring fairness in credit approval predictions.

Data Quality Validation Workflow

2.2.2 Model Behavior Testing

Model behavior testing is a critical step in validating the functionality, reliability, and robustness of AI systems. Unlike traditional software, which follows deterministic rules, AI models are probabilistic by nature. Their outputs depend on complex interactions between input data, underlying algorithms, and training processes. This makes rigorous testing essential to ensure models perform as expected not only under normal conditions but also when confronted with edge cases, noisy inputs, or adversarial challenges.

At its core, model behavior testing asks a fundamental question: How well does the model behave in the real world? It seeks to uncover vulnerabilities, assess generalization capabilities, and verify that the model's predictions align with established benchmarks. Without such testing, models risk underperforming, behaving unpredictably, or, in the worst cases, perpetuating biases that lead to harmful outcomes.

Key Objectives of Model Behavior Testing

The primary aim of model behavior testing is to verify that the system produces accurate and consistent results. For example, a fraud detection model should reliably flag high-risk transactions while ignoring legitimate ones. This level of consistency is key to maintaining trust in the system, particularly when it is deployed in high-stakes environments such as finance or healthcare.

Equally important is the ability to generalize. A model must perform well on unseen data that varies from its training set. For instance, a sentiment analysis model trained on customer reviews from the technology industry should also classify reviews from the hospitality sector with reasonable accuracy. Generalization ensures that the model is versatile and not overly tailored to a narrow dataset.

Another essential goal is identifying the model's weak points. Ambiguous inputs, such as idiomatic phrases for a text translation model, can expose areas where the system struggles. Testing for these weak points allows teams to refine the model, improving its resilience.

Finally, robustness testing evaluates how well the model performs under imperfect conditions, such as noisy, incomplete, or adversarial data. For instance, an image classification model should recognize objects even if the input image is slightly distorted. These tests simulate real-world imperfections to ensure the system can handle them gracefully.

Types of Model Behavior Testing

Model behavior testing encompasses a range of strategies, each designed to evaluate specific aspects of the system's performance. Validation against known outputs is one of the most fundamental methods. By testing the model on datasets with pre-labeled outputs, teams can measure metrics such as accuracy, precision, recall, and F1-score. For example, a cancer detection model might be evaluated against a labeled set of MRI scans to verify its predictions.

Explainability testing is another vital component, particularly for models deployed in sensitive domains like credit scoring or medical diagnostics. Techniques like SHAP (SHapley Additive exPlanations) or LIME (Local Interpretable Model-agnostic Explanations) help make the model's decisions interpretable. For instance, in a credit scoring system, explainability testing might reveal that "income" and "debt-to-income ratio" are the most influential factors in determining eligibility, ensuring stakeholders understand and trust the model's outputs.

Edge case testing challenges the model with inputs at the boundaries of expected conditions. A recommendation system, for example, might be tested using user profiles with minimal activity to evaluate how well it generates suggestions for such sparse data.

Adversarial testing introduces slight perturbations to inputs to assess the model's resilience. For instance, adding random noise to images fed into an object detection model can reveal vulnerabilities, helping to protect the system against malicious exploitation.

Finally, bias and fairness testing evaluates whether the model treats all demographic groups equitably. For example, a loan approval model might be tested to ensure it does not disproportionately reject applicants from specific demographics, addressing concerns about fairness and ethical AI practices.

Steps in Model Behavior Testing

Effective model behavior testing begins with defining clear benchmarks for performance. Teams must specify what constitutes success, such as achieving at least 85% accuracy on a test dataset. Once these expectations are established, testing scenarios are created to simulate a variety of conditions. These scenarios range from standard inputs to adversarial and edge cases.

For instance, consider an NLP model designed for customer support chatbots. It should be evaluated using clean datasets to verify baseline performance, as well as noisy datasets with misspellings and slang to test resilience. Additionally, the chatbot's ability to manage simultaneous conversations with multiple users should be tested to simulate real-world interaction patterns.

Analyzing the outputs from these tests is a critical step. Metrics such as the True Positive Rate and False Positive Rate for a binary classification model provide insights into its correctness and reliability. Weaknesses uncovered during this phase, such as underperformance on certain demographics or difficulty handling noisy inputs, inform iterative refinements. The model is retrained with additional data or adjusted algorithms to address these gaps, and the tests are rerun to validate improvements.

Tools for Model Behavior Testing

A variety of tools facilitate model behavior testing, making it more efficient and comprehensive. For explainability, SHAP and LIME help teams interpret predictions and ensure the model's decision-making aligns with stakeholder expectations. Adversarial robustness toolkits like Foolbox enable teams to simulate perturbations and test model resilience against attacks. Meanwhile, libraries like Scikit-learn provide metrics for performance evaluation, such as confusion matrices and classification reports. These tools collectively enhance the rigor and precision of testing workflows.

The Value of Model Behavior Testing

Model behavior testing is more than a technical exercise—it is a safeguard for ensuring AI systems are reliable, fair, and effective in the real world. By rigorously evaluating models under diverse conditions, teams can identify weaknesses, mitigate risks, and instill confidence in end-users. Whether ensuring that a fraud detection system minimizes false positives or validating the fairness of a loan approval model, behavior testing forms the backbone of trustworthy AI development.

As AI systems continue to influence critical decisions in industries ranging from healthcare to finance, the importance of robust model behavior testing cannot be overstated. It is through these meticulous efforts that AI can achieve its transformative potential while upholding the principles of accuracy, fairness, and reliability.

Example in Practice

Imagine a facial recognition system developed for a security application. Its performance depends on its ability to identify individuals across varying conditions, such as different demographics, lighting scenarios, and image quality levels. To ensure robustness, the model undergoes extensive testing.

First, it is evaluated on datasets with balanced demographics to identify any biases in accuracy across groups. Variations in lighting and image clarity are then introduced to test how well the model adapts to imperfect conditions. Finally, adversarial examples, such as images with minor pixel modifications, are used to assess whether the system is vulnerable to manipulation.

Based on these tests, the team identifies areas for improvement. For example, accuracy for underrepresented demographics may lag, prompting adjustments to the training dataset. Similarly, the model's robustness against adversarial inputs might require algorithmic refinements. These iterative improvements result in a system that is both fairer and more resilient, aligning with the high stakes of its security-focused deployment.

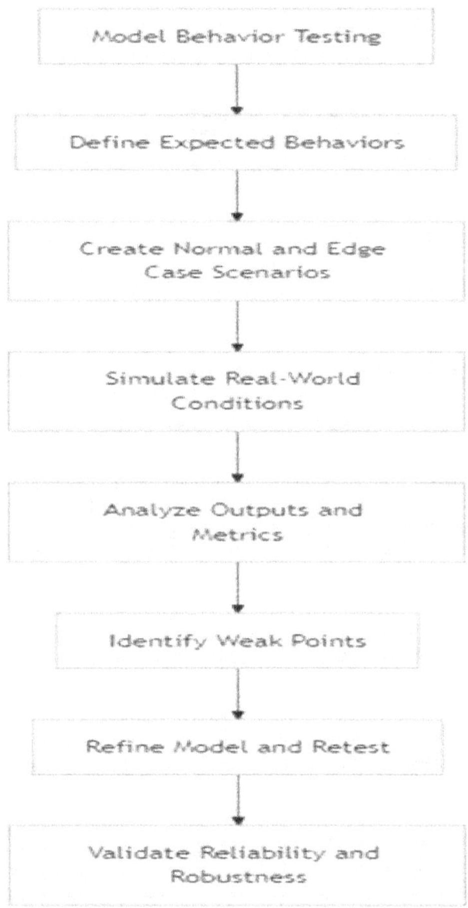

Model Behavior Testing Workflow

2.2.3 Performance Testing at Scale

AI systems are often deployed in environments where reliability and responsiveness are non-negotiable. Whether it's a recommendation engine that needs to suggest products in real-time or a fraud detection system scanning thousands of transactions per second, performance testing at scale is the linchpin that ensures these systems can handle the demands of production-level workloads. Unlike functional testing, which verifies that a system works as intended under typical conditions, performance testing pushes the boundaries—evaluating how well the system performs under stress, heavy loads, and extended usage.

Performance testing is not just about identifying weaknesses; it's about building confidence. By simulating realistic, and often extreme, scenarios, developers can uncover bottlenecks, optimize resource usage, and ensure seamless experiences for end-users. This process is vital for meeting service-level agreements (SLAs), reducing downtime risks, and enhancing user satisfaction.

Key Objectives of Performance Testing

At its core, performance testing aims to validate the efficiency and reliability of an AI system under varying conditions. One of the primary measures is **latency**—the time it takes for the system to respond to user requests. For instance, a recommendation engine on an e-commerce platform should generate personalized suggestions within 100 milliseconds. Delays beyond this can frustrate users, particularly during high-traffic events like Black Friday sales.

Another critical aspect is **scalability**. Scalability testing assesses whether the system can handle increasing workloads without a drop in performance. Consider a chatbot for customer service: it may perform flawlessly with a handful of users but must maintain the same level of responsiveness when managing thousands of concurrent conversations during a flash sale.

Throughput, or the number of tasks a system can process per second, is equally important. For example, a fraud detection system used by a major bank must analyze thousands of transactions every second during peak hours, ensuring fraudulent activities are flagged in real-time.

Lastly, performance testing identifies **bottlenecks**—those system components that impede overall performance. Perhaps an inefficient API call slows down a real-time prediction system, or a poorly optimized database query increases response times. By detecting these issues early, teams can implement targeted optimizations that dramatically improve system performance.

Common Scenarios for Performance Testing

Performance testing encompasses various scenarios designed to replicate real-world conditions, and sometimes to push beyond them. Stress testing, for example, deliberately overloads the system to identify breaking points. Imagine simulating a sudden surge of user activity on a streaming platform's search feature, mimicking the spike that occurs during the release of a blockbuster movie. Stress testing helps pinpoint when and where the system might fail under such conditions.

Load testing, by contrast, evaluates how well the system handles both normal and peak workloads. A demand forecasting model for a retail chain might be tested against historical sales data from all regional warehouses at once to ensure stability.

For systems prone to sudden fluctuations in usage, spike testing replicates abrupt increases and decreases in workload. A customer service chatbot, for instance, could be tested for its ability to handle a sharp influx of queries during a promotional campaign.

Finally, soak testing assesses long-term performance by running the system continuously over an extended period. This type of testing is invaluable for identifying issues like memory leaks in a predictive maintenance system, where prolonged use could otherwise degrade performance.

Steps in Performance Testing

The performance testing process begins with defining clear metrics to evaluate system performance. These metrics might include latency, throughput, and resource utilization, depending on the system's objectives. For example, a fraud detection system might have a performance target of processing 500 transactions per second with a response time under 50 milliseconds.

Once metrics are established, synthetic workloads are generated to simulate real-world conditions. For instance, datasets with millions of records might be used to evaluate a recommendation system's ability to process large volumes of data without compromising speed or accuracy.

Testing under realistic environments is crucial to obtaining meaningful results. This often involves deploying the system in a cloud environment that mirrors the production setup, ensuring that any issues identified during testing are relevant to actual deployment scenarios.

During testing, teams monitor metrics to detect performance bottlenecks. Tools like Grafana and Prometheus are commonly used to visualize key metrics such as API response times and GPU utilization, making it easier to identify problem areas. Once bottlenecks are identified, optimizations—such as refining database queries or adjusting load-balancing configurations—are implemented. The system is then retested to confirm that these changes have resolved the issues.

Tools for Performance Testing

A suite of tools is available to facilitate performance testing for AI systems. Locust, for example, is an open-source tool that simulates user traffic to evaluate system responsiveness under load. For more comprehensive load testing, JMeter can measure how many concurrent transactions a fraud detection API can handle while maintaining accuracy.

For real-time data streaming, Apache Kafka provides an excellent framework to evaluate how well a predictive maintenance system processes continuous input from IoT devices. Meanwhile, Grafana and Prometheus allow teams to monitor and visualize system performance metrics over time, making them indispensable for soak testing and long-duration analysis.

Benefits of Performance Testing

Performance testing is not just a technical exercise—it is a commitment to delivering seamless, reliable, and scalable AI solutions. By ensuring systems operate efficiently under real-world conditions, performance testing builds trust with end-users and stakeholders alike.

Whether it's a chatbot that must manage thousands of simultaneous conversations, a predictive maintenance system monitoring machinery in real-time, or a recommendation engine processing millions of requests during a flash sale, performance testing ensures these systems are up to the task. With the right strategies, tools, and commitment to optimization, AI systems can achieve their full potential, delighting users and driving meaningful results for organizations.

Example in Practice

Consider a retail e-commerce platform deploying an AI-powered recommendation engine designed to provide real-time product suggestions. During high-traffic events like Black Friday, the system must process thousands of requests per second while maintaining sub-100ms response times.

To ensure readiness, performance testing simulates user requests at varying loads, starting with 1,000 requests per second and scaling to 10,000. Metrics such as response times, recommendation accuracy, and GPU utilization are monitored throughout the test.

During the initial tests, significant delays are observed at higher loads. Upon investigation, the team identifies inefficiencies in the database query logic that slow down data retrieval. After optimizing the queries, the system's response times improve by 50%, enabling it to handle peak traffic seamlessly.

This rigorous testing not only ensures the recommendation engine performs reliably during critical events but also enhances user satisfaction by delivering fast, relevant suggestions, even under heavy loads.

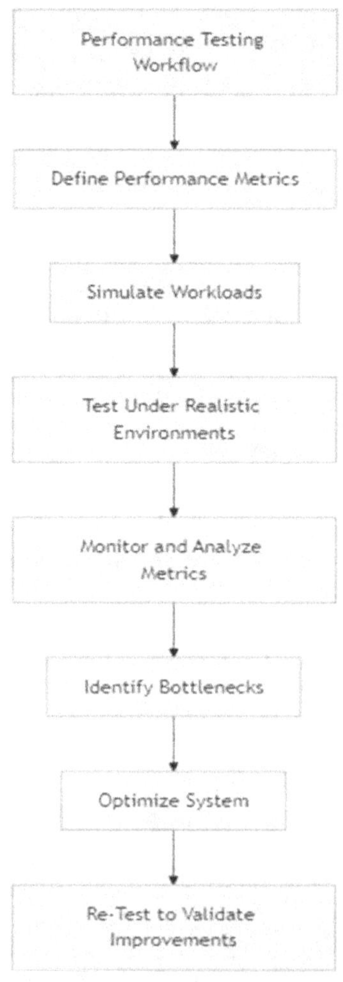

Performance Testing Workflow

2.3 Automated Testing Pipeline

As AI systems grow in complexity, ensuring consistent quality across their development and deployment lifecycle becomes both a necessity and a challenge. Automated testing pipelines have emerged as a cornerstone of modern AI quality assurance, providing a structured and scalable approach to validate data, models, and system interactions. These pipelines, seamlessly integrated into Continuous Integration and Continuous Deployment (CI/CD) workflows, not only reduce the burden of manual testing but also enable teams to identify and address issues at the earliest possible stage.

An automated testing pipeline acts as a vigilant gatekeeper, ensuring that every piece of the AI system, from the data it ingests to the predictions it generates, meets predefined standards. By embedding automation into testing processes, organizations can accelerate development cycles, maintain reliability, and adapt to the dynamic nature of AI systems.

Key Components of an Automated Testing Pipeline

The foundation of an effective automated testing pipeline is the integration of tests at every stage of the AI lifecycle. This includes data validation, model performance checks, integration testing, and deployment validation. Each of these components plays a crucial role in maintaining system integrity and ensuring the AI solution performs as intended.

Data validation is the first line of defense in any AI system. Since models are only as good as the data they're trained on, ensuring the quality of incoming data is non-negotiable. Automated data validation scripts, powered by tools like Great Expectations, can detect anomalies, missing values, and invalid formats. For example, a daily data ingestion pipeline might automatically check that all columns in a dataset are complete and fall within expected ranges before allowing the data to proceed further.

Next, **model validation** ensures that models meet performance expectations after training or updates. Automated tests can evaluate metrics such as precision, recall, and F1-score, flagging any deterioration in performance. This step is particularly critical for AI systems that are retrained frequently, such as a recommendation engine that adjusts its predictions based on real-time user behavior. By automating these evaluations, teams can ensure models remain reliable and aligned with project goals.

Integration testing validates the seamless interaction between system components. In AI workflows, this might involve verifying that APIs serving model predictions handle various input scenarios correctly or ensuring that data flows smoothly from preprocessing pipelines into training modules. Tools like Postman can automate API tests, simulating diverse requests to ensure the system responds accurately and consistently.

Finally, **deployment testing** focuses on validating the behavior of models in staging or production environments. For instance, a chatbot deployment might undergo automated tests to evaluate response accuracy, latency, and the ability to handle edge cases before being exposed to end-users.

Building and Running the Pipeline

Creating an automated testing pipeline requires careful planning and the integration of robust tools. The process typically begins with the incorporation of data validation tests. Scripts are written to check for issues such as missing values, inconsistencies, or biases in the incoming data. For example, a fraud detection system might validate that all transactions include necessary attributes like timestamp, amount, and location before processing them for training or predictions.

Model testing is then added to the pipeline. Libraries like Pytest allow developers to create scripts that automatically evaluate model performance against predefined benchmarks. These scripts ensure that any new model iteration maintains or improves upon critical metrics like accuracy or recall.

Integration tests are essential for ensuring that individual components work together harmoniously. Tools like Postman can automate the testing of APIs, validating that they return correct outputs for a variety of input scenarios. For example, a sentiment analysis API might be tested to confirm it handles edge cases like ambiguous or sarcastic phrases appropriately.

The pipeline culminates in deployment testing, where the entire system is evaluated in an environment that mirrors production. Here, tools like TensorFlow Extended (TFX) can validate both data and models during pipeline execution, ensuring smooth transitions from staging to live deployment.

To maximize efficiency, these testing stages are embedded into CI/CD workflows. Platforms like GitHub Actions or Jenkins can trigger tests automatically whenever new code or data is pushed, generating detailed logs and reports for review. Visualization tools like Allure provide clear, actionable insights into test outcomes, helping teams quickly identify and resolve failures.

Benefits of Automated Testing Pipelines

The value of automated testing pipelines lies in their ability to deliver consistent quality at scale. By identifying issues early—whether in data preprocessing, model training, or system integration—these pipelines reduce the risk of costly failures in production. They also free teams from repetitive manual tasks, allowing them to focus on innovation and refinement.

Automation ensures that every update, whether to data, models, or workflows, is rigorously validated against standardized tests. This consistency not only maintains system reliability but also fosters confidence among stakeholders. Moreover, the rapid feedback provided by automated pipelines accelerates development cycles, enabling teams to iterate on AI models with greater efficiency.

Example in Practice

To illustrate the impact of automated testing pipelines, consider a financial institution deploying an AI-powered fraud detection system. This system ingests daily transaction data, validates it, processes it through machine learning models, and returns predictions to identify potentially fraudulent activities.

The automated pipeline begins with a data validation stage. Tools like Great Expectations check for missing or anomalous records, ensuring the data is complete and accurate. Next, model performance is evaluated using automated scripts that test metrics like precision and recall on updated datasets. Integration tests validate that the API serving fraud predictions handles various input scenarios correctly, including edge cases like unusually large transactions. Finally, deployment tests confirm that the system maintains response times and accuracy under production-like conditions.

By implementing this pipeline, the institution reduces manual intervention by 70% while ensuring continuous quality. The system remains robust, even as data evolves and models are retrained, providing reliable fraud detection at scale.

The Road Ahead: Scalable and Reliable AI Systems

Automated testing pipelines are more than a quality assurance tool—they are a strategic investment in the long-term success of AI systems. By embedding rigorous, repeatable checks into every stage of the AI lifecycle, organizations can build solutions that are not only technically sound but also reliable, scalable, and aligned with user expectations.

As AI continues to evolve, so too will the demands placed on these systems. With automated testing pipelines in place, teams are better equipped to meet these challenges, delivering high-quality AI solutions that inspire confidence and drive meaningful outcomes.

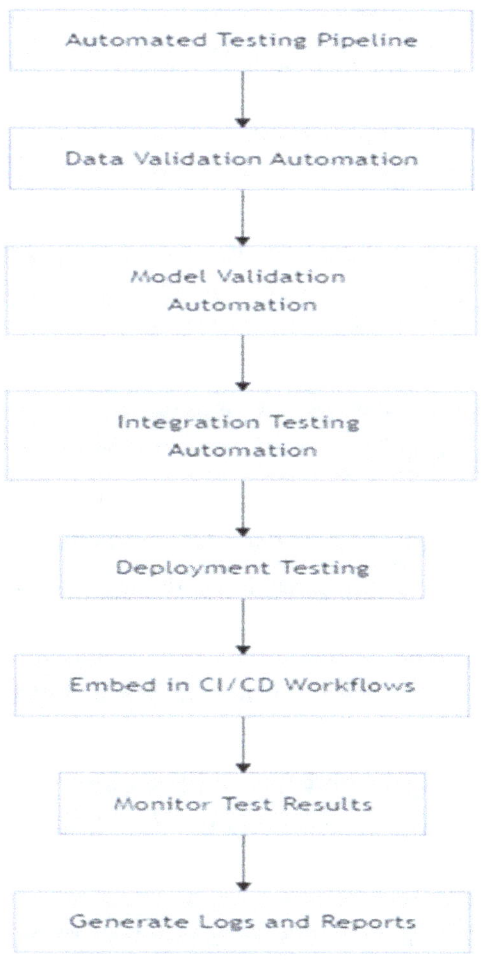

Automated Testing Pipeline

2.3.1 CI/CD for AI Systems

In the fast-evolving landscape of artificial intelligence, maintaining efficiency and reliability is as critical as the innovations themselves. Continuous Integration and Continuous Deployment (CI/CD) pipelines are the engines that drive this efficiency, enabling organizations to keep pace with iterative model improvements, dynamic data updates, and evolving deployment environments. While traditional software development has long benefited from CI/CD methodologies, AI systems demand a more nuanced approach—one that accounts for the complexities of data dependencies, algorithmic updates, and real-world variability.

A well-architected CI/CD pipeline for AI does more than streamline workflows; it ensures that every change, whether in code, data, or model architecture, is rigorously validated and seamlessly deployed. This is about more than automation; it's about embedding quality and reliability into the very fabric of the development process.

Building Blocks of an AI-Focused CI/CD Pipeline

The foundation of a CI/CD pipeline for AI systems lies in its ability to unify and automate the lifecycle of data, models, and system integration. Version control, automated testing, continuous integration, and continuous deployment come together to create a robust framework for managing AI workflows.

At its core, version control enables teams to manage changes systematically. While tools like Git have long been staples for managing source code, AI projects introduce additional layers of complexity—datasets and models evolve just as much as the underlying code. Specialized tools like DVC (Data Version Control) allow teams to track changes in datasets alongside their code counterparts. Imagine a team working on a fraud detection system. As new types of fraud emerge, both the training dataset and model logic must adapt. Version control ensures that these changes are tracked cohesively, preserving the integrity of the system's history.

Automated testing is another cornerstone of the pipeline. For AI systems, testing extends beyond traditional unit tests for code. Data quality checks, model performance validations, and integration tests are all vital. Consider a recommendation engine updating daily based on user interactions. Automated tests validate that incoming data is clean and representative, that the updated model meets performance thresholds, and that the API serving predictions responds accurately. These tests ensure that changes enhance the system without introducing regressions.

Continuous integration takes this a step further by automatically merging updates into the main branch, provided they pass all tests. For instance, a team tweaking hyperparameters in a model might push their changes to a feature branch. CI tools like Jenkins or GitHub Actions can trigger a series of validations, ensuring the updated model not only performs better but integrates seamlessly with other system components.

Finally, continuous deployment automates the transition from testing to production. Here, the pipeline evaluates the readiness of a model for deployment, ensuring it meets performance and reliability criteria before rolling it out. A retail pricing optimization system might deploy updated models daily, but only if they demonstrate consistent improvements in revenue projections during staging tests. Kubernetes, a popular orchestration tool, simplifies this process by managing containerized deployments, ensuring scalability and resource efficiency.

Steps to Implement an AI CI/CD Pipeline

The journey to an effective CI/CD pipeline begins with establishing strong version control practices. Teams typically use Git for code and augment it with tools like MLflow or DVC to manage datasets and models. A practical example is a financial institution developing a risk assessment model. By committing code changes and corresponding dataset updates to a unified repository, the team ensures transparency and reproducibility.

Next, automated testing stages are introduced to validate every component. These stages encompass data validation scripts to flag anomalies, model evaluation scripts to measure accuracy and fairness, and integration tests to verify API interactions. For instance, a language model API might undergo rigorous tests to ensure it handles ambiguous phrases without errors, safeguarding the user experience.

To ensure consistency, the pipeline incorporates containerization. Tools like Docker allow developers to package models with all their dependencies, enabling reproducibility across development, staging, and production environments. This is particularly valuable for collaborative projects where team members work on different configurations. A predictive maintenance system, for instance, can be deployed consistently across edge devices and cloud platforms thanks to containerization.

The CI workflow orchestrates these steps, triggering automated validations with every new commit. Whether it's a preprocessing script update or a major model overhaul, CI tools ensure that all changes are vetted systematically. Once a change passes these checks, the CD workflow takes over, deploying the model to a staging environment. This allows stakeholders to validate its impact in real-world conditions before promoting it to production.

Finally, monitoring systems provide continuous feedback, tracking deployed models for accuracy, drift, and performance. If a fraud detection model's precision drops below a defined threshold, for example, the system can trigger an alert or even initiate retraining automatically.

Tools for CI/CD in AI Systems

1. **GitHub Actions**:

    ○ Automates CI/CD workflows for code, data, and models.

    ○ Example: Automatically test and deploy an NLP model upon merging a pull request.

2. **Jenkins**:

    ○ Flexible CI/CD tool for building, testing, and deploying AI pipelines.

    ○ Example: Create a pipeline to validate and deploy a computer vision model.

3. **DVC (Data Version Control)**:
   - Tracks dataset and model versions, ensuring reproducibility.
   - Example: Automatically switch between dataset versions for specific branches.
4. **MLflow**:
   - Manages the ML lifecycle, including tracking experiments and deploying models.
5. **Kubernetes**:
   - Orchestrates containerized deployments, scaling resources as needed.

Why CI/CD Matters for AI

The benefits of implementing a CI/CD pipeline for AI are multifaceted. By automating repetitive tasks and embedding validation into every stage, teams can iterate faster, ensuring that improvements reach production without unnecessary delays. Reproducibility is another significant advantage, as the pipeline tracks every change, allowing teams to roll back or replicate results when needed.

Quality and reliability are also enhanced. Automated checks catch issues early, reducing the risk of deploying underperforming models. This is particularly important for AI systems where errors can have significant consequences, such as in healthcare diagnostics or financial decision-making.

A Practical Example: Pricing Optimization in Retail

To see the impact of CI/CD in action, consider a retail company using AI to optimize product pricing. The system ingests sales data, updates its model, and generates new price recommendations daily.

In this scenario, version control tracks changes to the training scripts and sales data. Automated tests validate that the incoming data is complete and consistent and that the updated model achieves better revenue predictions. The CI workflow merges updates only if all tests pass, while the CD workflow deploys the validated model to a staging environment for stakeholder review. Once approved, the model goes live, influencing pricing decisions across thousands of products.

Monitoring systems track the model's accuracy and business impact, ensuring it remains effective. If accuracy drops or the model shows signs of drift, the pipeline initiates retraining, keeping the system aligned with current market trends.

By automating these processes, the retailer reduces manual intervention, accelerates model updates, and maintains a competitive edge.

A Foundation for Scalable AI

CI/CD pipelines for AI are more than just a set of automated tasks—they are a framework for innovation. They empower teams to focus on creativity and problem-solving by offloading routine tasks to a reliable system. As AI continues to grow in complexity and impact, these pipelines will be the backbone of scalable, efficient, and trustworthy solutions. Through CI/CD, organizations can ensure that their AI systems not only meet today's needs but are ready to adapt to the challenges of tomorrow.

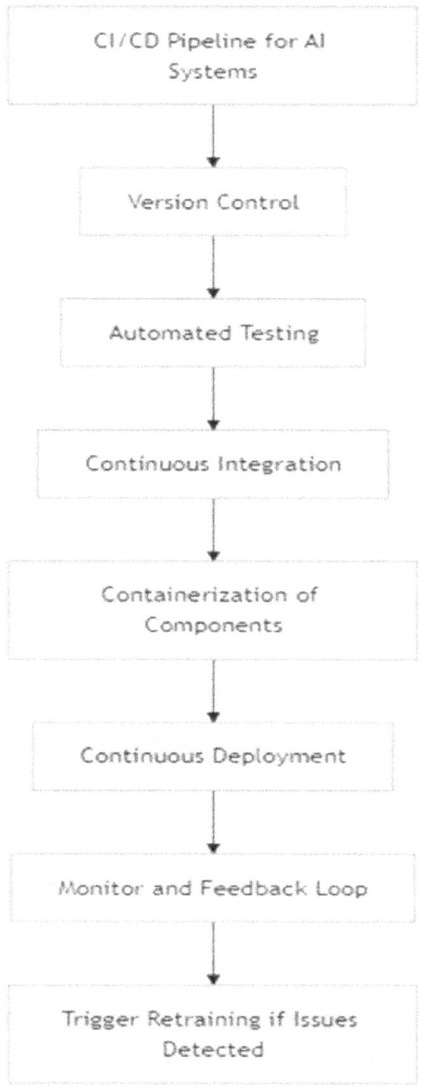

CI/CD Pipeline for AI Systems

2.3.2 Automated Test Cases

Automated test cases form the backbone of a robust AI testing pipeline, reducing manual effort and ensuring consistent quality across workflows. These test cases are pre-defined scripts or configurations designed to validate specific aspects of the AI system, such as data quality, model performance, and system integration. By automating repetitive testing tasks, teams can accelerate development cycles while maintaining high-quality standards.

Key Types of Automated Test Cases

1. **Data Validation Tests**:
   - Automates checks for data consistency, completeness, and accuracy.

- Example: Ensure that all numeric columns in a dataset fall within expected ranges.

2. **Model Performance Tests**:

   - Validates the performance of models against pre-defined metrics like accuracy, precision, and recall.

   - Example: Automatically evaluate a classification model to ensure it achieves at least 85% accuracy on the test dataset.

3. **Integration Tests**:

   - Automated testing of interactions between components, such as APIs, databases, and models.

   - Example: Verify that an API endpoint serving model predictions processes input JSON correctly and returns valid responses.

4. **Stress and Load Tests**:

   - Simulates high workloads to evaluate system stability under stress.

   - Example: Test a fraud detection API by sending a high volume of concurrent requests.

5. **Regression Tests**:

   - Ensures that updates to code or models do not break existing functionality.

   - Example: Re-run automated tests on a recommendation system after retraining it with updated data.

Steps to Create Automated Test Cases

1. **Define Test Objectives**:

   - Clearly specify what each test case aims to validate.

   - Example: A test case for data validation might ensure that no column has more than 1% missing values.

2. **Select or Create Datasets**:

   - Use synthetic, mock, or real-world datasets to create test scenarios.

   - Example: Generate a synthetic dataset with edge cases to test model robustness.

3. **Write Test Scripts**:

   - Develop scripts for each test case using programming languages or testing frameworks.

   - Example: Use Python with libraries like pytest for model evaluation.

4. **Automate Execution**:

   - Schedule automated test execution using CI/CD pipelines.

- Example: Integrate tests with Jenkins to trigger them on every code commit.

5. **Log Results and Generate Reports**:
   - Capture test outcomes and highlight failures for debugging.
   - Example: Use tools like Allure to visualize pass/fail rates for all automated test cases.

Tools for Creating Automated Test Cases

1. **Great Expectations**:
   - Framework for automating data validation checks.
   - Example: Validate that a time-series dataset has no missing timestamps.

2. **Pytest**:
   - Python-based framework for creating and running automated tests.
   - Example: Automate regression tests for a machine learning model.

3. **Selenium**:
   - Automates browser-based UI tests.
   - Example: Test an AI-powered dashboard for data visualization accuracy.

4. **Apache JMeter**:
   - Simulates load and stress conditions for APIs.
   - Example: Test an NLP-based chatbot under concurrent user interactions.

Benefits of Automated Test Cases

1. **Increased Efficiency**:
   - Reduces manual testing time and accelerates development cycles.

2. **Consistent Quality**:
   - Ensures all updates meet standardized validation criteria.

3. **Early Bug Detection**:
   - Identifies issues early in the pipeline, minimizing downstream failures.

4. **Scalability**:
   - Easily adapts to larger datasets or more complex systems as the project scales.

5. **Comprehensive Coverage**:
   - Provides consistent validation across various scenarios, from normal to edge cases.

Example in Practice

Consider an AI-powered anomaly detection system for network security:

- **Scenario**: The system identifies unusual traffic patterns in real-time to flag potential security threats.

- **Test Cases**:

  1. **Data Validation**: Ensure incoming traffic logs have no missing IP addresses or timestamps.

  2. **Model Performance**: Validate that the anomaly detection model achieves a minimum recall of 90%.

  3. **Integration Tests**: Verify that flagged anomalies are correctly routed to a dashboard via an API.

  4. **Stress Test**: Simulate high traffic volumes to ensure the system maintains response times under 100ms.

- **Outcome**: Automated test cases streamline validation, ensuring the system reliably detects anomalies without manual intervention.

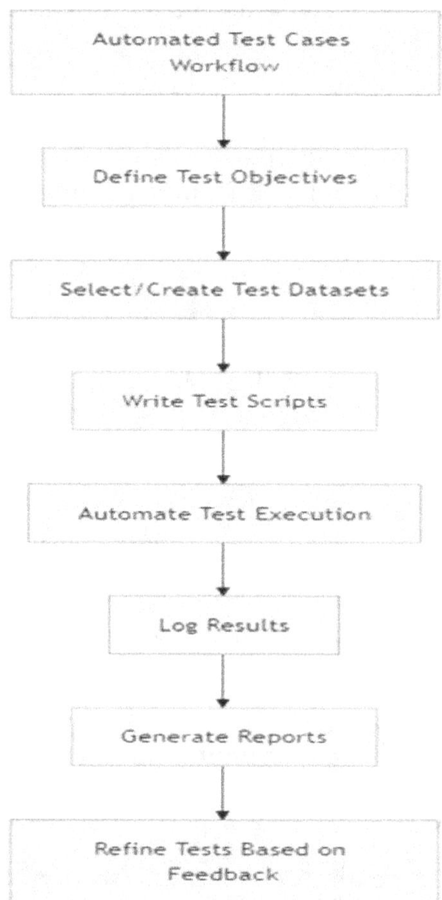

Automated Test Cases Workflow

2.3.3 Testing Tools & Frameworks

In the ever-evolving landscape of AI development, automated test cases are the unsung heroes that underpin reliability and scalability. By systematically validating data, models, and system interactions, these test cases ensure that AI systems meet high standards of performance and accuracy—every time. Instead of relying on labor-intensive, manual checks, automated tests allow teams to focus on innovation while ensuring their systems remain robust, even as they grow more complex.

Automated test cases are more than a productivity tool—they are the backbone of quality assurance. They provide the consistency needed to validate complex AI workflows, from raw data ingestion to model inference and system integration. By embedding these tests into development pipelines, teams can identify and resolve issues early, prevent regressions, and maintain user trust in the system's reliability.

Key Categories of Testing Tools & Frameworks

Automated test cases are tailored to validate specific aspects of AI systems. Let's explore how these tests safeguard different stages of development:

Data Validation Tests

Data is the lifeblood of AI systems, but it's often messy, incomplete, or inconsistent. Automated data validation tests ensure that datasets meet predefined quality standards before they are used for training or inference. For instance, a test might check that numeric columns in a dataset fall within an acceptable range, preventing errors caused by outliers or invalid entries.

Consider an AI-powered sales forecasting model. If product categories are missing from the dataset, the model might struggle to provide accurate predictions. A data validation test could detect this issue, flagging the dataset for correction before it progresses through the pipeline.

Model Performance Tests

AI models are only as good as their performance metrics. Automated performance tests measure critical factors like accuracy, precision, recall, and F1-score, ensuring that models meet or exceed predefined benchmarks. For instance, a test could evaluate whether a classification model achieves at least 85% accuracy on a validation dataset.

These tests are invaluable for systems where precision matters. In healthcare, for example, a cancer detection model must consistently identify malignancies with high recall, ensuring no cases are overlooked.

Integration Tests

AI systems are rarely standalone entities. They interact with APIs, databases, and user interfaces, forming a network of interdependent components. Integration tests validate that these interactions work seamlessly, ensuring that data flows correctly and that outputs align with expectations.

Imagine an API serving predictions from a recommendation model. Integration tests could simulate various payloads to confirm that the API processes inputs and returns accurate results without errors, even under edge cases.

Stress and Load Tests

AI systems often face unpredictable workloads, especially in production. Stress and load tests simulate these conditions, ensuring that systems remain stable under heavy traffic or processing demands. For instance, a fraud detection API might be tested with thousands of concurrent requests to validate its ability to maintain low response times.

Such tests are critical during high-stakes scenarios, like Black Friday sales for e-commerce platforms, where user demand can surge unexpectedly.

Regression Tests

AI systems are iterative by nature, constantly updated with new data or improved algorithms. Regression tests ensure that these updates don't inadvertently break existing functionality. For example, after retraining a recommendation model with updated data, regression tests would re-validate previous workflows, ensuring consistent quality across iterations.

Popular Testing Tools for AI Systems

In the intricate ecosystem of AI systems, the right tools and frameworks can be the difference between a seamless deployment and a cascade of failures. As AI models grow more complex and workflows increasingly dynamic, leveraging specialized tools for testing ensures that systems remain robust, efficient, and scalable. These tools automate and streamline testing tasks, from data validation to API integration, offering a structured approach to quality assurance. Below, we explore some of the most widely used tools and frameworks that have become indispensable for AI testing.

Great Expectations: Setting Data Standards

Data lies at the heart of every AI system, and ensuring its quality is non-negotiable. Great Expectations is a tool purpose-built for data validation, enabling teams to define and enforce rules for completeness, uniqueness, and consistency. It acts like a vigilant gatekeeper, flagging any irregularities before they impact downstream processes.

For example, consider an AI system predicting customer lifetime value. If the dataset contains missing values in critical columns like "age" or "purchase history," the predictions could be skewed. Great Expectations enables teams to set up automated checks to catch these issues, generating detailed reports that highlight where the data fails to meet expectations.

MLflow: Tracking the Machine Learning Lifecycle

AI systems are dynamic, often requiring retraining, hyperparameter tuning, and model experimentation. MLflow simplifies this lifecycle management by tracking model metrics, parameters, and artifacts across multiple iterations. Its ability to integrate with popular frameworks like TensorFlow and PyTorch makes it a versatile choice for machine learning projects.

Imagine a scenario where a team retrains a recommendation engine monthly to incorporate new user data. MLflow can automatically log performance metrics like precision and recall for each iteration, ensuring that newer models consistently outperform their predecessors. This level of tracking not only improves accountability but also facilitates collaborative workflows across teams.

Postman: Ensuring API Integrity

Modern AI systems often interact with users or other systems through APIs. Postman excels at testing these interfaces, simulating real-world scenarios with customizable payloads. It's particularly useful for regression tests, ensuring that API endpoints continue to function as expected even after updates.

Take an AI-driven recommendation engine deployed via an API. Postman can simulate user requests to validate that the system delivers accurate recommendations within acceptable response times. By automating these tests, teams can catch potential issues early, ensuring a smooth user experience.

Selenium: Automating Web Interface Testing

Many AI systems include user-facing dashboards or visualization tools. Selenium is a powerful framework for automating browser-based testing, simulating user interactions like clicks, form submissions, and navigation. It's ideal for validating that web-based analytics platforms correctly display AI-generated insights.

For instance, an AI-powered healthcare dashboard might visualize patient readmission risks. Selenium can automate tests to ensure that risk scores, trends, and alerts are rendered accurately, verifying that the system delivers actionable insights without glitches.

JMeter: Stress Testing for Performance

AI systems are often deployed in environments with unpredictable workloads. JMeter excels at stress and load testing, simulating high-concurrency scenarios to measure system performance under pressure. By identifying bottlenecks and weaknesses, it ensures systems can handle real-world demands.

Picture a chatbot API designed to assist thousands of users during a product launch. Using JMeter, teams can simulate this peak traffic, measuring latency and throughput to ensure the system doesn't falter when it matters most.

TensorFlow Extended (TFX): Orchestrating AI Pipelines

For end-to-end AI workflows, TensorFlow Extended (TFX) is a comprehensive platform that automates data preprocessing, model validation, and deployment. It ensures that each stage of the pipeline meets predefined standards before progressing, making it invaluable for large-scale machine learning systems.

Consider a company deploying an image recognition model for quality control in manufacturing. TFX can validate that retrained models achieve required accuracy thresholds before deployment, ensuring consistent performance across production environments.

Frameworks for Automated Testing

Pytest: Versatility in Testing

Pytest is a Python-based framework that excels in unit and integration testing. Its support for mocking and parameterized testing makes it particularly suited for AI systems, where multiple components interact dynamically. For example, Pytest can automate regression tests for feature extraction scripts, ensuring consistency in preprocessing pipelines.

Robot Framework: End-to-End Testing Made Simple

Robot Framework is a general-purpose testing framework that integrates with tools like Selenium for comprehensive testing. It's particularly effective for end-to-end validations, such as ensuring a customer service chatbot performs reliably across various scenarios.

Apache Airflow: Workflow Validation

Apache Airflow orchestrates machine learning pipelines, automating tasks like data preprocessing, model training, and evaluation. By embedding validation steps directly into Airflow's Directed Acyclic Graphs (DAGs), teams can ensure that each stage meets quality standards before moving forward.

Steps to Implement Testing Tools in AI Projects

The journey to a robust testing strategy begins with understanding the system's requirements. For AI projects heavily reliant on data, tools like Great Expectations are essential to ensure datasets meet stringent quality benchmarks. Conversely, systems with complex integrations might prioritize Postman for API validation or Selenium for user interface testing.

Once the tools are selected, integrating them into CI/CD pipelines is crucial for automation. For instance, Jenkins or GitHub Actions can trigger these tools to run tests automatically whenever new code or data is pushed, ensuring continuous validation. Teams should regularly monitor test results to identify and address bottlenecks, using insights to optimize workflows.

Benefits of Testing Tools & Frameworks

Testing tools and frameworks significantly enhance both the quality and efficiency of AI development. By automating repetitive tasks, they free up valuable time for teams to focus on innovation. Centralized platforms like MLflow enable better collaboration, while performance-oriented tools like JMeter ensure systems are ready for real-world challenges.

For instance, consider a healthcare AI system predicting patient readmission risks. The system ingests hospital records, preprocesses data, trains models, and serves predictions through APIs. Using tools like Great Expectations for data validation, MLflow for performance tracking, and Postman for API testing, the development team can ensure that each component meets its respective quality standards. JMeter adds another layer of assurance, validating the system's scalability during high-traffic periods. Together, these tools streamline development and safeguard reliability.

In the fast-paced world of AI, testing tools are more than just quality assurance—they are enablers of innovation. They allow teams to build complex systems with confidence, knowing that each component, from data pipelines to user interfaces, has been rigorously validated. By incorporating these tools into automated workflows, organizations can achieve the dual goals of agility and reliability, delivering AI solutions that perform flawlessly, even under the most demanding conditions.

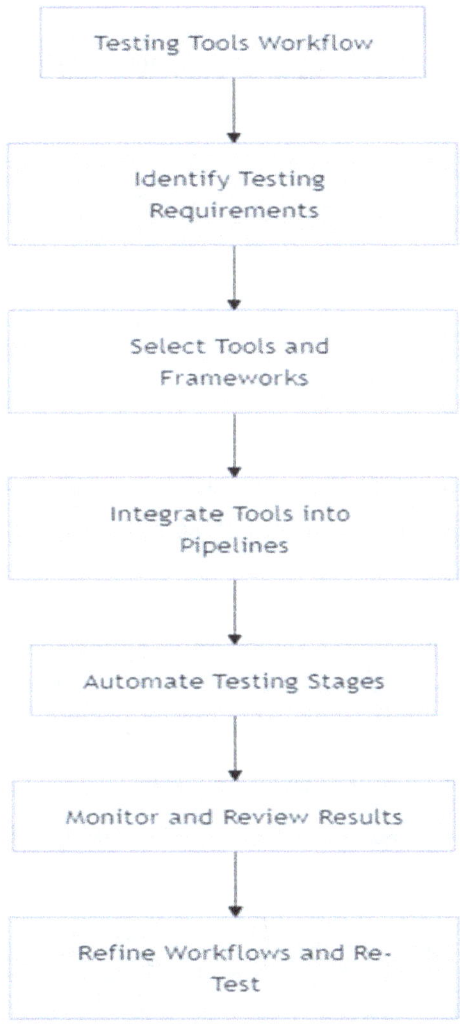

Testing Tools Workflow

2.4 Quality Metrics & Monitoring

Maintaining the reliability of AI systems in production environments hinges on careful monitoring and evaluation. Unlike traditional software, where performance is more predictable, AI systems operate in dynamic conditions. Their effectiveness can shift over time due to evolving data distributions, user interactions, and external factors like workload variations. Implementing robust quality metrics and monitoring frameworks helps teams detect issues early, mitigate risks, and ensure ongoing alignment with performance expectations. This chapter explores key quality metrics for AI systems, strategies for monitoring, and the tools that make it all possible.

Key Quality Metrics for AI Systems

To understand the performance and impact of an AI system, monitoring must cover several critical dimensions. These include the accuracy of predictions, the consistency of incoming data, system responsiveness, and the business outcomes the AI solution enables.

Model Performance Metrics

At the heart of any AI system are the predictions it generates. Metrics like accuracy, precision, recall, and F1-score measure the model's ability to make correct decisions, often reflecting how well it performs on tasks like classification, regression, or clustering.

For instance, consider a fraud detection system. Precision ensures the system minimizes false positives, reducing the number of legitimate transactions flagged incorrectly. Recall measures its ability to catch fraudulent transactions. A balance between these metrics, captured in the F1-score, ensures the system delivers optimal performance under real-world conditions.

Data Quality Metrics

The quality of data flowing into the system is as critical as the performance of the model itself. Metrics here evaluate completeness, consistency, and representativeness to ensure that the model processes reliable and relevant information.

Take a retail forecasting system as an example. Timeliness in data ingestion is essential—sales data must be as current as possible to ensure predictions reflect the latest trends. If records contain missing values for key features like product categories or regions, predictions may be skewed, highlighting the need for robust data quality checks.

System Performance Metrics

Non-functional aspects of the system, such as latency, throughput, and scalability, often define the user experience. These metrics measure the system's efficiency in delivering results, especially under varying loads.

A recommendation engine serving millions of users during a high-traffic event, like Black Friday, must keep latency under 100 milliseconds to ensure seamless interactions. Monitoring throughput helps teams confirm that the system can process a high volume of requests per second without degradation.

Business Impact Metrics

Ultimately, AI systems exist to achieve specific business goals. Metrics tied to revenue growth, customer satisfaction, and cost efficiency gauge the tangible value these systems deliver. For example, a customer support chatbot might be evaluated on how much it reduces operational costs while improving user satisfaction scores.

Steps for Implementing Quality Monitoring

A robust monitoring framework begins with aligning on what matters most to the system and its stakeholders. Establishing metrics alone isn't enough; teams need to continuously track them, act on deviations, and iteratively improve.

Defining Key Metrics

Collaborating with stakeholders ensures the monitoring framework reflects both technical and business priorities. For example, an anomaly detection system might prioritize recall to ensure it captures all critical anomalies, paired with a focus on minimizing false alarms.

Establishing Baseline Thresholds

Historical data or industry benchmarks can help set thresholds for acceptable performance. For instance, a sentiment analysis model might require a minimum accuracy of 85% to meet customer service standards. These baselines provide a reference point for identifying deviations.

Integrating Monitoring Tools

Effective monitoring relies on tools that capture and visualize metrics in real time. Dashboards like those provided by Grafana can track trends such as API latency or data drift, allowing teams to spot patterns and anomalies at a glance.

Continuous Monitoring and Alerts

Monitoring must be automated and proactive. Alerts notify teams when performance falls below thresholds, enabling quick responses. For example, an alert might trigger if a fraud detection model's recall drops below 90%, signaling a potential issue with recent data quality or model drift.

Iterative Improvements

No system is static. Regular analysis of monitoring data helps teams identify opportunities to retrain models, refine workflows, or optimize infrastructure. For instance, if accuracy declines in a sentiment analysis model due to emerging slang, retraining on updated datasets can restore performance.

Tools for Monitoring Quality Metrics

A suite of specialized tools supports quality monitoring in AI systems. These tools range from tracking data quality and model performance to monitoring system health.

Evidently AI

Evidently AI simplifies the tracking of data and model performance. It can detect data drift by monitoring feature distributions, sending alerts if new data diverges significantly from training data. For example, a churn prediction system might flag changes in customer demographics that could affect model reliability.

Grafana and Prometheus

These tools combine real-time metrics collection with powerful visualization capabilities. Prometheus can log API response times, while Grafana provides dashboards to view trends like throughput and latency, ensuring system performance stays on track.

MLflow

For tracking the lifecycle of machine learning models, MLflow excels. It logs metrics, parameters, and model artifacts, making it easier to compare different iterations. For instance, teams can identify the most effective version of a model based on its performance across datasets.

DataDog

DataDog focuses on infrastructure monitoring, tracking resource utilization such as CPU and GPU usage. It's especially useful for ensuring deployed AI systems remain performant during high-traffic periods.

Benefits of Quality Metrics & Monitoring

Implementing robust quality metrics and monitoring frameworks provides organizations with several key advantages.

1. **Early Detection of Issues** Monitoring can catch problems like model drift, latency spikes, or data inconsistencies before they impact users. For instance, identifying a shift in data distribution early can prevent performance drops in production.

2. **Continuous Improvement** Insights from monitoring enable teams to iteratively refine models, workflows, and infrastructure. This proactive approach ensures AI systems remain accurate and efficient over time.

3. **Alignment with Business Goals** By tying metrics to tangible outcomes like revenue growth or customer satisfaction, monitoring ensures AI systems deliver measurable value aligned with organizational priorities.

4. **Building Trust** Reliable monitoring frameworks instill confidence in end-users and stakeholders, demonstrating that the system performs fairly and consistently.

Example in Practice

Consider an AI-powered credit risk assessment system at a bank. The system evaluates loan applications and generates risk scores. To ensure it performs effectively, the bank implements a comprehensive monitoring strategy:

- **Model Metrics:** Precision and recall are tracked to minimize false approvals and ensure high-risk applicants are flagged correctly.

- **Data Quality Metrics:** Incoming financial records are validated to ensure completeness and relevance.

- **System Metrics:** API latency is monitored to ensure risk scores are delivered within 500 milliseconds.

- **Business Metrics:** Metrics such as reduced loan defaults and improved approval times reflect the system's impact.

Over time, continuous monitoring reveals a seasonal trend in loan application data, prompting the team to retrain the model. This adaptation maintains accuracy and fairness, reinforcing trust in the system.

Monitoring quality metrics in AI systems is not just a safeguard; it's an enabler of growth and reliability. By continuously tracking and responding to key metrics, organizations can ensure their AI systems remain robust, scalable, and aligned with both technical and business objectives. The dynamic nature of AI demands vigilance, but with the right metrics, tools, and processes, teams can confidently navigate the complexities of production AI.

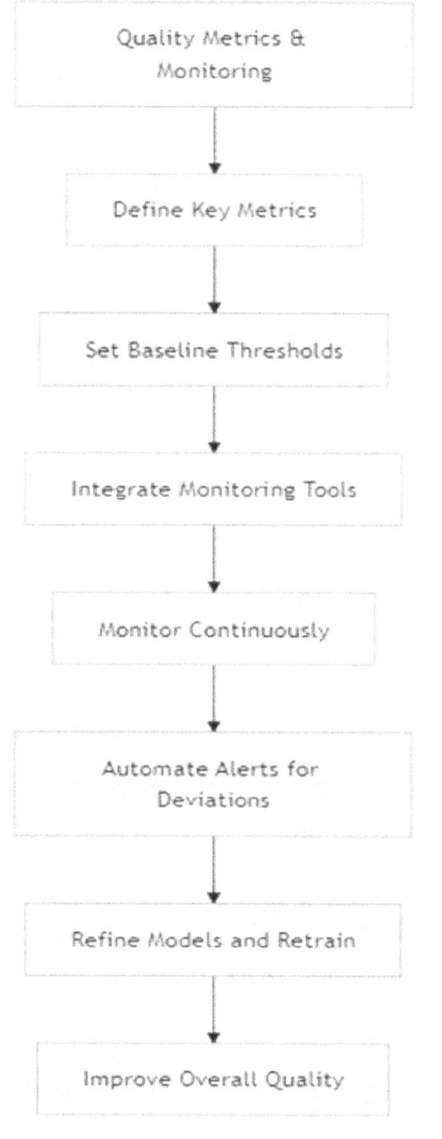

Quality Metrics & Monitoring Workflow

2.4.1 Performance Monitoring

Performance monitoring in AI systems ensures that models and workflows operate effectively under real-world conditions. Unlike pre-deployment testing, which often unfolds in controlled environments, performance monitoring assesses the behavior of AI systems in dynamic, production scenarios. It involves tracking key metrics—such as latency, throughput, error rates, and resource utilization—to ensure the system meets both user expectations and organizational objectives. This process is not just about maintaining system efficiency; it's also about creating a feedback loop to sustain and improve performance over time.

Key Objectives of Performance Monitoring

AI systems in production face challenges that extend beyond their training environment. They interact with unpredictable data, evolving workloads, and often, external systems with their own complexities. Without robust performance monitoring, these systems can falter—whether through increased latency, degraded accuracy, or outright failures. The goal of performance monitoring is to catch these issues early, optimize operations, and ensure the system performs as reliably under stress as it does under normal conditions.

Detecting Performance Degradation

Degradation can manifest in various ways, such as longer response times or reduced model accuracy. For example, an AI-powered recommendation engine might exhibit slower API response times during high traffic periods. Monitoring tools can track this latency in real-time, allowing teams to intervene before users are affected.

Resource Optimization

Efficient use of computational resources is critical, especially for models running in cost-sensitive environments. Performance monitoring helps track resource utilization across CPUs, GPUs, memory, and storage, ensuring that resources are neither underutilized nor overtaxed. For instance, a predictive maintenance model running on edge devices must stay within memory constraints to avoid crashing or disrupting workflows.

Tracking Data Drift

AI models rely on data, but when the incoming data diverges significantly from the training data—a phenomenon known as data drift—their performance can suffer. Monitoring can flag changes in data distributions, such as shifts in customer behavior in an e-commerce platform, enabling teams to adapt the system proactively.

Ensuring Scalability

AI systems must handle variable workloads, from routine operations to peak demands. For example, during a flash sale, a fraud detection API might experience a surge in transaction volumes. Monitoring the system's scalability ensures it can handle such spikes without performance degradation.

Key Metrics for Performance Monitoring

Effective performance monitoring requires a focus on metrics that reflect both system health and user experience. These metrics should be actionable, providing clear insights into where improvements are needed.

- **Latency** measures how quickly the system responds to queries or inputs. For instance, a chatbot designed to assist customers should process and return responses within 300 milliseconds to maintain a conversational flow.

- **Throughput** captures the system's ability to handle workloads, such as the number of predictions or tasks completed per second. A real-time image processing system, for example, might be required to process at least 50 images per second to meet operational needs.

- **Error Rates** reveal how often the system produces incorrect results or fails to process requests. For a loan approval model, tracking prediction errors ensures the system minimizes false negatives, protecting both users and business interests.

- **Resource Utilization** monitors the system's consumption of computational and storage resources. A deep learning model deployed on cloud servers, for instance, should avoid GPU overloading during peak usage to prevent interruptions.

- **Model Drift** measures changes in data or prediction distributions over time. Monitoring a customer churn model, for example, can help detect shifts in prediction accuracy due to seasonal behavior changes.

Steps to Implement Performance Monitoring

Establishing an effective monitoring framework involves several deliberate steps, each aimed at ensuring that no aspect of the system's performance goes unchecked.

Identifying Critical Metrics

Collaborate with stakeholders to define metrics that are essential to the system's success. For instance, in an inventory management AI system, the focus might be on ensuring prediction accuracy while maintaining API latency below a set threshold.

Setting Thresholds and Alerts

Define acceptable ranges for each metric and configure alerts to trigger when deviations occur. For example, an alert might notify the team if a model's accuracy drops below 85% or if an API response time exceeds 500 milliseconds.

Integrating Monitoring Tools

Choose tools that align with the system's architecture and performance goals. Combining Prometheus for metric collection and Grafana for visualization, for example, creates a powerful solution for tracking latency, throughput, and resource usage in real-time.

Automating Data Collection

Automation ensures that monitoring happens consistently and without manual intervention. Pipelines can be configured to log metrics like inference times and prediction errors for historical analysis.

Analyzing Trends and Acting

Performance monitoring is not just about real-time insights; it's also about identifying patterns over time. For instance, a periodic spike in latency might indicate inefficiencies in query handling, prompting targeted optimizations.

Tools for Performance Monitoring

A range of tools can streamline the process of tracking and visualizing AI system performance:

- **Prometheus** is widely used for collecting and querying performance metrics, making it ideal for monitoring API response times or model inference latency.

- **Grafana** provides customizable dashboards that visualize trends in key metrics, such as throughput and resource usage.

- **Evidently AI** focuses on monitoring model performance and data drift, offering insights into how data shifts may affect accuracy.

- **DataDog** tracks infrastructure performance, including CPU and GPU usage, ensuring smooth operation of resource-intensive models.

- **AWS CloudWatch** offers system-level monitoring tailored to cloud-based deployments, tracking failures and processing times in serverless architectures.

Benefits of Performance Monitoring

Implementing performance monitoring delivers tangible advantages, ensuring the long-term health and reliability of AI systems:

- **Early Detection of Issues**: By identifying bottlenecks and anomalies before they impact users, monitoring prevents minor issues from escalating into major problems.

- **Optimized Resource Allocation**: Insights into resource utilization help teams allocate compute and storage resources efficiently, reducing costs.

- **Enhanced Scalability**: Monitoring validates that the system can handle fluctuating workloads without compromising performance, ensuring resilience during high-demand periods.

- **Improved User Experience**: By maintaining responsiveness and accuracy, performance monitoring safeguards the system's usability and reliability.

Example in Practice

Imagine a streaming service using an AI-powered recommendation engine. The system generates real-time recommendations based on users' viewing histories. To ensure it performs optimally, the team implements a robust performance monitoring strategy:

- **Latency** is tracked to ensure recommendations appear within 200 milliseconds of a user action.

- **Throughput** is monitored to confirm the system serves thousands of recommendations per second.

- **Resource Utilization** is measured, with GPU usage observed to avoid overloading during peak hours.

- **Model Drift** is checked to identify shifts in user preferences over time.

Over time, the team observes a spike in latency during evening hours. By optimizing the recommendation algorithm and fine-tuning resource allocation, they reduce latency by 30%, improving the overall user experience.

Performance monitoring is a vital component of maintaining AI systems in production. It enables teams to address issues proactively, optimize resource usage, and sustain a seamless user experience. With the right metrics, tools, and strategies in place, organizations can ensure their AI systems deliver reliable, scalable, and impactful results in any real-world environment.

Performance Monitoring Workflow

2.4.2 Alert Design & Management

The reliability of AI systems in production depends heavily on the ability to detect and address issues swiftly. This is where well-crafted alert design and management play a crucial role. Alerts act as the system's early warning mechanism, notifying teams of deviations in performance, data integrity, or resource usage before these issues escalate into critical failures. Thoughtful alerting not only minimizes downtime but also ensures that AI systems deliver consistent and high-quality results in dynamic environments.

The Importance of Thoughtful Alert Design

Alerts are the eyes and ears of an AI system in production. When designed effectively, they serve as invaluable tools that empower teams to address potential problems proactively. However, poorly structured alerts—either too frequent or too sparse—can create challenges. Over-alerting leads to noise, causing teams to ignore even critical notifications. Under-alerting, on the other hand, risks missing vital issues.

The ultimate goal of alert management is to strike a balance: notifications should be timely, actionable, and prioritized according to their impact. For instance, a latency spike in an AI model serving API predictions might not immediately disrupt operations, but it serves as an early indicator that demands attention. Conversely, a data pipeline failure warrants immediate escalation due to its potential to halt downstream processes.

Core Objectives in Alert Design

Effective alerts achieve more than just reporting errors; they provide clarity, context, and resolution pathways.

Timely Detection

The first goal of an alert is to notify the right team as soon as an issue is detected. For example, if an API serving model predictions experiences a latency increase beyond 500 milliseconds, the alert should reach the relevant engineers immediately. Early detection allows teams to intervene before the issue affects users or business operations.

Minimized Noise

Alert fatigue can be just as damaging as no alerts at all. Teams overwhelmed by false positives or low-priority alerts may begin ignoring notifications altogether. A well-designed alert minimizes noise by carefully calibrating thresholds and incorporating contextual insights. For instance, minor fluctuations in model accuracy that remain within an acceptable range should not trigger alerts, allowing teams to focus on significant deviations instead.

Actionable Insights

An alert should guide the recipient toward resolution. Including diagnostic information, such as recent metric trends, error logs, or impacted system components, transforms the alert into a tool for action. For example, an alert for increased memory usage might include details about specific processes consuming excess resources, helping engineers pinpoint the issue quickly.

Prioritization

Not all issues require the same level of urgency. Alerts should differentiate between critical failures—such as a model producing invalid predictions—and lower-priority concerns, like a temporary increase in latency during peak hours. For instance, a data pipeline failure might be classified as critical, triggering escalation protocols, while a minor API latency increase is logged as a warning.

Types of Alerts for AI Systems

AI systems operate across interconnected layers of data, computation, and deployment infrastructure, each requiring targeted monitoring.

1. **Performance Alerts** These alerts focus on the system's responsiveness and efficiency. For example, if 10% of requests to a prediction model exceed 200 milliseconds in latency, a performance alert can flag this deviation, ensuring service levels remain consistent.

2. **Data Drift Alerts** AI models are highly sensitive to changes in data distributions. A drift in key features, such as user demographics in a recommendation system, can significantly degrade performance. Alerts for such shifts ensure teams can retrain or recalibrate models as needed.

3. **Model Degradation Alerts** Over time, models may lose accuracy or reliability due to changes in input data or evolving conditions. For instance, an alert might notify teams if the precision of a classification model drops below 85% over consecutive prediction batches.

4. **Infrastructure Alerts** These alerts monitor the system's computational backbone. For example, if GPU utilization exceeds 90% for an extended period, the system might trigger an alert to prevent overload and potential downtime.

Steps to Design Effective Alerts

Identify Metrics that Matter

Designing meaningful alerts begins with identifying the key metrics that reflect the health and performance of the system. For instance, a fraud detection model might prioritize metrics such as precision, recall, and API latency.

Set Meaningful Thresholds

Defining thresholds for alerts requires careful consideration of the system's normal operating range. These thresholds should balance sensitivity and specificity, avoiding unnecessary alerts while capturing critical deviations. For example, an API error rate exceeding 1% for more than five minutes might justify an alert, whereas brief fluctuations can be ignored.

Prioritize Notifications

Not all alerts demand the same response. Categorizing notifications into severity levels—such as critical, warning, and informational—ensures that teams focus their efforts where it matters most.

Choose the Right Channels

Different alerts require different notification methods. Low-priority warnings might be routed to a Slack channel, while critical failures escalate through PagerDuty to ensure immediate action.

Automate Escalation

Unresolved issues can escalate automatically. For example, if a GPU overload alert goes unaddressed for 30 minutes, it might be routed to engineering leadership to expedite resolution.

Test and Refine

Regularly simulate scenarios to evaluate the effectiveness of alerts and adjust thresholds as necessary. Stress testing, for instance, can reveal whether latency alerts trigger appropriately during load spikes.

Tools for Alert Design & Management

The tools an organization chooses for managing alerts significantly influence how effectively it can monitor and respond to potential issues in AI systems. Tools like **Prometheus and Grafana** excel at collecting real-time metrics and presenting them in visually intuitive dashboards, making them ideal for tracking key indicators such as latency spikes or throughput declines. **PagerDuty**, on the other hand, is designed for escalation and resolution, ensuring that critical notifications reach the appropriate personnel quickly and with minimal friction. For teams needing a more comprehensive solution, **DataDog** offers infrastructure and application monitoring capabilities, which can range from tracking model accuracy drops to identifying increased CPU usage. If the system operates in a cloud environment, **AWS CloudWatch** provides detailed monitoring and alerting, tailored specifically for cloud-based infrastructure and applications.

Benefits of Effective Alert Management

Effective alert management transforms how teams maintain system health, leading to substantial operational advantages. When alerts are thoughtfully designed, they help teams detect and resolve issues early, significantly minimizing user disruptions. For example, an early-warning system that highlights API latency increases can allow engineers to resolve bottlenecks before they affect users, ensuring smoother operations.

Beyond reducing downtime, alerting systems enhance the overall reliability of AI systems. Continuous monitoring ensures that the system remains stable even under fluctuating workloads or unexpected conditions. Well-designed alerts also streamline the troubleshooting process, offering actionable insights that reduce the time required to diagnose and resolve issues. Instead of starting from scratch, teams can focus directly on the identified problem.

Additionally, effective alert management contributes to team productivity. By eliminating unnecessary or redundant notifications, alert systems prevent "alert fatigue" and allow team members to concentrate on critical tasks. Prioritizing high-impact alerts over minor fluctuations ensures that attention is directed where it matters most.

A Real-World Illustration: An AI Chatbot in Action

Consider an AI-powered chatbot designed to manage customer inquiries across multiple regions and languages. As the system scales to handle thousands of queries per minute, ensuring consistent performance becomes critical. This is where an effective alert management strategy proves invaluable.

Alerts can be configured to track several key metrics. For instance, **performance alerts** notify the team if the chatbot's response time exceeds 500 milliseconds. This could indicate an underlying bottleneck that needs immediate investigation. At the same time, **model degradation alerts** might trigger if the chatbot's intent recognition accuracy drops below 85%, signaling that the system's ability to understand user queries is deteriorating. Similarly, **infrastructure alerts** can monitor the chatbot servers, flagging cases where memory usage exceeds 80%, preventing potential crashes during peak traffic.

By implementing such a system, the organization can maintain the chatbot's performance even under heavy loads. During a peak usage period, these alerts enabled the engineering team to address issues proactively, reducing user complaints by 20%. This not only enhanced the user experience but also ensured that the system continued to meet service-level expectations.

The Broader Implications of Thoughtful Alert Management

In production environments, alert design and management are more than just tools—they are essential components of a robust AI operations strategy. By helping teams navigate complexities like performance monitoring, model degradation, and infrastructure health, well-designed alerts foster confidence in the system's reliability.

To achieve this, organizations should focus on crafting alerts that are actionable, timely, and prioritized. Noise should be minimized, ensuring that teams can trust the alerting system to provide relevant and urgent notifications. By implementing scalable tools and integrating them into their workflows, organizations can keep their AI systems running efficiently, even in the face of evolving demands and unexpected challenges.

Effective alert management doesn't just protect systems; it empowers teams to focus on innovation and growth, knowing that their infrastructure is secure, reliable, and well-monitored.

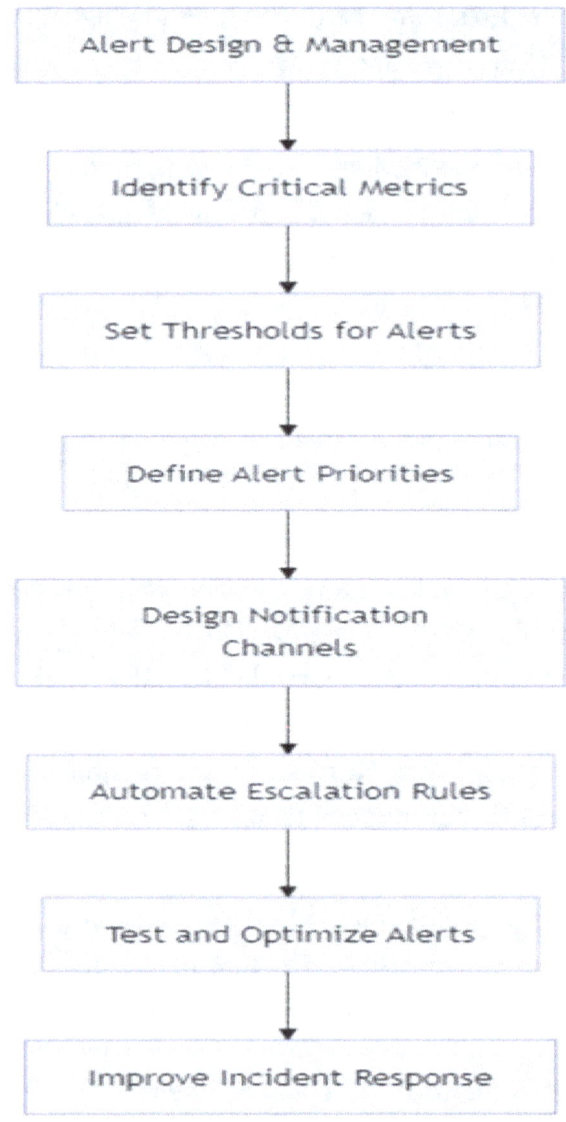

Alert Design & Management Workflow

2.4.3 Quality Gates & Criteria

Quality gates and criteria are indispensable tools in the AI development lifecycle, serving as structured checkpoints that evaluate whether systems meet established benchmarks before progressing to subsequent stages. These gates function as both safeguards and enablers, ensuring that AI models, data, and workflows align with predefined standards of performance, compliance, and reliability. By integrating quality gates, organizations can mitigate risks, prevent substandard deployments, and uphold the trustworthiness of their AI systems.

The Purpose of Quality Gates in AI Systems

The primary objective of quality gates is to create a framework for systematic validation, ensuring consistency and reliability across every phase of development. For example, before a recommendation engine is deployed to production, it should be rigorously evaluated against a minimum F1-score threshold—ensuring it delivers accurate and meaningful results to users. Without such controls, organizations risk deploying flawed models that could undermine user trust or business objectives.

Beyond technical validation, quality gates are crucial for enforcing compliance with ethical and regulatory standards. In a healthcare application, for instance, a model might need to demonstrate adherence to data privacy laws such as HIPAA. These requirements can be baked into the quality gate criteria, ensuring that ethical considerations are integrated into the technical workflows rather than treated as an afterthought.

Standardization is another key benefit of implementing quality gates. By applying uniform validation criteria across data processing scripts, model training pipelines, and deployment workflows, teams can maintain consistency in their outputs. Such standardization is vital, especially in collaborative environments where multiple stakeholders are responsible for different components of the system.

Finally, quality gates reduce operational risks by catching issues early in the pipeline. Consider a time-series dataset intended for a forecasting model. If the data contains inconsistencies—such as irregular timestamps—these issues can propagate, leading to inaccurate predictions. A quality gate that validates data integrity before it is used in model training can avert such downstream errors.

Building and Implementing Quality Gates

The successful implementation of quality gates begins with clearly defining the criteria at each stage of the workflow. These criteria should be specific and measurable, tied to the system's goals. For instance, a fraud detection model might require a recall rate of at least 90% to ensure that most fraudulent transactions are caught. Similarly, latency requirements for an API could mandate response times below 50 milliseconds during peak usage.

Automation plays a critical role in embedding quality gates into the AI pipeline. Tools such as Great Expectations allow teams to automate data quality checks, verifying attributes like completeness and consistency before datasets proceed to the next phase. For model validation, platforms like MLflow can track performance metrics and enforce thresholds, blocking the promotion of underperforming models.

Integrating these gates into CI/CD workflows ensures that validation occurs seamlessly with every update. For example, a Jenkins pipeline might automatically halt progress if a model fails to meet established accuracy benchmarks during testing. This continuous validation approach not only reduces manual intervention but also accelerates the iteration cycle, allowing teams to focus on refining their solutions.

Logging and reviewing the results of quality gates is equally important. Detailed logs help identify recurring bottlenecks, such as a persistent drop in model accuracy when handling certain data subsets. Visualization tools like Grafana can make these metrics accessible, enabling stakeholders to quickly diagnose and address issues.

Tools Supporting Quality Gate Implementation

Several tools are tailored to the task of implementing quality gates in AI systems. Great Expectations, for instance, specializes in data validation, ensuring datasets meet predefined standards before they are processed. MLflow, meanwhile, provides a robust framework for tracking model metrics, configurations, and artifacts, ensuring alignment with performance thresholds. For orchestrating pipelines, Apache Airflow can automate tasks like data validation, model evaluation, and deployment, embedding quality gates into the workflow. Additionally, tools like Evidently AI offer capabilities to monitor data and model drift, validating that production inputs remain consistent with training data distributions.

Practical Benefits and Real-World Application

Quality gates deliver tangible benefits across the AI lifecycle. By enforcing consistent validation criteria, they prevent the deployment of suboptimal models or workflows, minimizing the risk of failures in production. This consistency also enhances trust among stakeholders, who can be confident that every system deployed meets rigorous standards.

Moreover, automating these processes accelerates iteration cycles, enabling teams to focus on innovation rather than repetitive manual checks. This is particularly important in dynamic fields like AI, where rapid prototyping and refinement are key to staying competitive.

Consider a real-world example of an AI-powered loan approval system. In this case, quality gates can be applied at multiple levels. A data quality gate ensures that customer profiles are complete, with no missing values in critical fields like income or credit scores. A model performance gate might block deployment if the model's recall rate for identifying eligible applicants falls below 92%, ensuring the system minimizes missed opportunities. System integration gates validate API response times, ensuring they remain under 200 milliseconds even during high traffic. Finally, a deployment gate might include a bias audit, confirming that no demographic group is disproportionately rejected.

The result of these quality gates is a system that performs reliably, complies with ethical standards, and meets business objectives. By catching issues early and enforcing consistent validation, the organization ensures the system operates effectively while minimizing risks.

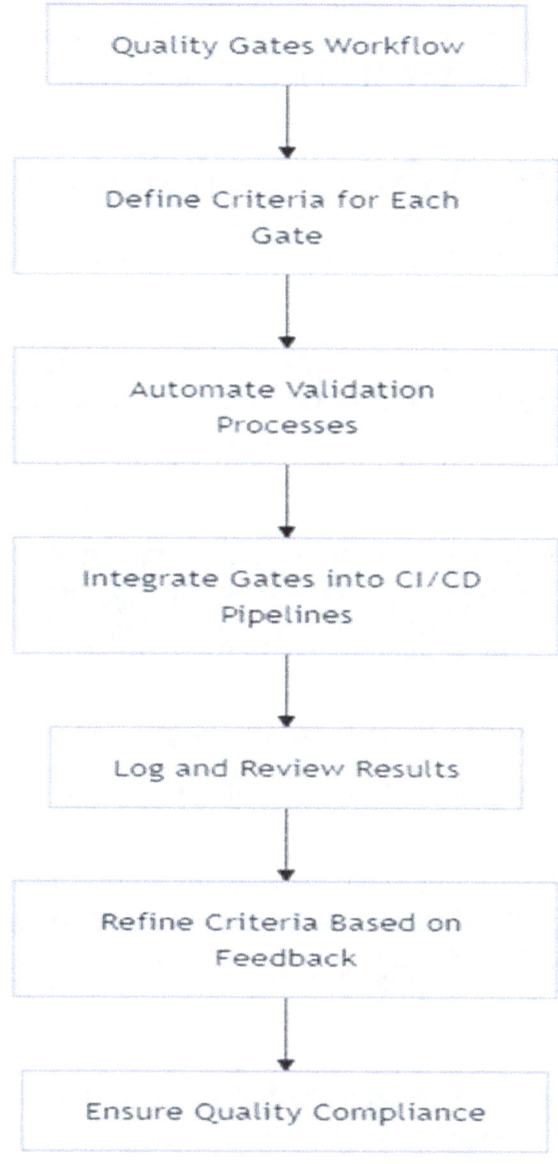

Quality Gates Workflow

Quality gates and criteria are not just checkpoints—they are foundational pillars of robust AI development. By implementing structured validations, organizations can prevent costly errors, standardize processes, and maintain the reliability of their systems. Tools and automation further enhance the effectiveness of these gates, embedding quality assurance into every phase of the AI lifecycle. In doing so, teams can confidently deploy AI systems that deliver value, uphold ethical standards, and stand resilient against the complexities of real-world environments.

Chapter 3

HRIS Solution Architecture

3.1 Modern HRIS Architecture Patterns

The landscape of Human Resource Information Systems has undergone a remarkable transformation over the past decade. As organizations grapple with increasingly complex HR processes and the demand for more agile, responsive systems, traditional monolithic architectures have given way to more sophisticated approaches. This evolution reflects not just technological advancement, but a fundamental shift in how we think about managing human capital in the digital age.

3.1.1 Microservices Architecture

In the early days of HRIS, systems were built as monolithic applications – massive, self-contained programs that handled everything from payroll to performance reviews. While these systems worked, they were like enormous ocean liners: powerful but difficult to maneuver. Any change, no matter how small, required careful consideration of the entire system's integrity. Adding new features was like trying to renovate a house while still living in it – complicated, risky, and often disruptive.

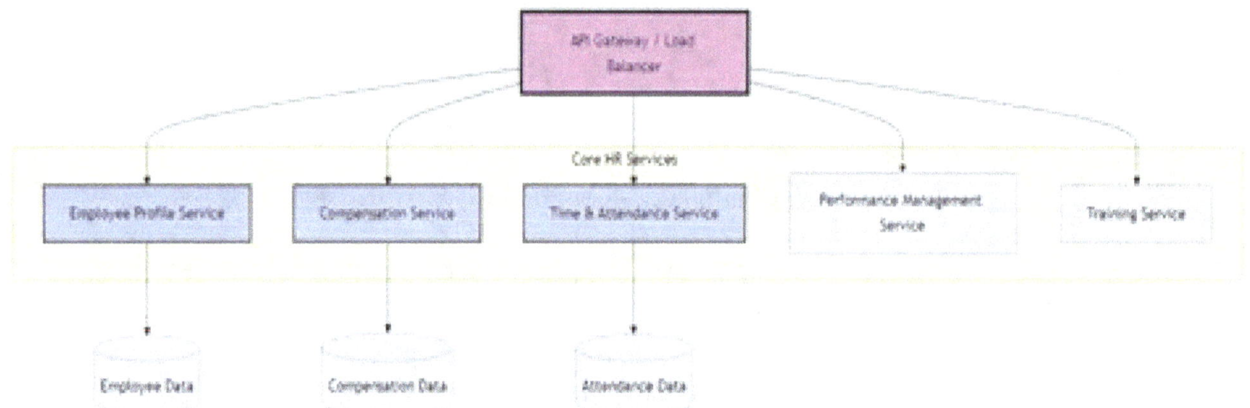

Consider the employee onboarding process in a modern HRIS. When a new hire joins the organization, multiple systems need to spring into action. The Employee Profile Service creates the basic employee record, while the Compensation Service sets up salary information. Simultaneously, the Training Service begins preparing the onboarding curriculum, and the Time & Attendance Service establishes leave balances and work schedules.

Service boundaries in microservices architecture require careful consideration. Take the example of employee skills management. Should it reside in the Employee Profile Service or the Training Service? The decision depends on your organization's specific needs. Some companies implement a dedicated Skills Service when they realize that skills data is crucial for both profile management and training initiatives. This flexibility to evolve and adapt is a key strength of microservices architecture.

Data consistency across services presents unique challenges. When an employee transfers departments, multiple services need updating. Modern HRIS implementations handle this through event-driven architecture. The Employee Profile Service publishes a "DepartmentTransfer" event, which other services consume and process according to their specific needs. This decoupling ensures system resilience while maintaining data consistency.

Performance optimization in microservices requires thoughtful caching strategies. Global Industries, a multinational corporation, implemented distributed caching for their employee profile data. This reduced database load and improved response times for their globally distributed workforce. They used Redis clusters strategically placed in different regions, ensuring fast access to frequently requested data while maintaining data consistency through careful cache invalidation strategies.

3.1.2 API-First Design

Modern HRIS solutions adopt an API-First approach, fundamentally changing how we build and integrate HR systems. This philosophy prioritizes the API design as the first and most crucial step in system development, rather than treating it as an afterthought.

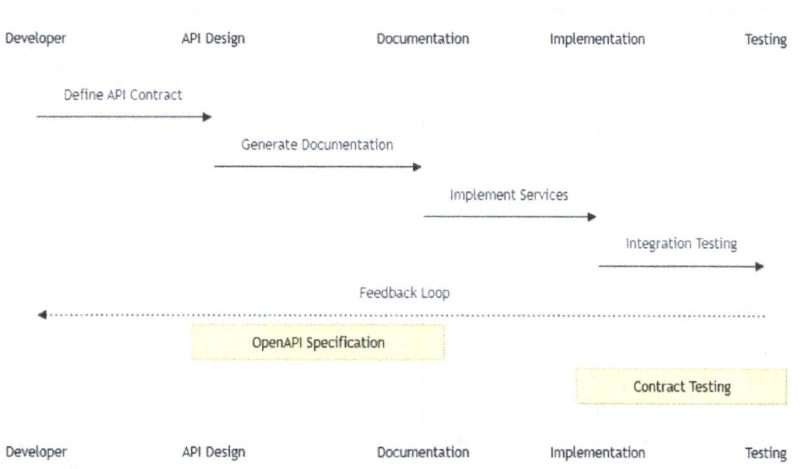

The journey of implementing API-First design begins with comprehensive API contracts. These contracts serve as the single source of truth for all system interactions. Consider how TechCorp revolutionized their HRIS by starting with detailed API specifications. Their contract included not just endpoint definitions but also robust error handling, rate limiting policies, and data validation rules.

Authentication and authorization in API-First design require sophisticated approaches. Modern HRIS implementations typically use OAuth 2.0 with JWT (JSON Web Tokens) for secure access control. This allows fine-grained permission management – a crucial requirement for HR systems where data privacy is paramount. For instance, a manager might have access to their team's attendance records but not their salary information.

Version management becomes critical in API-First design. When FastTrack HR needed to update their compensation calculation algorithms, they maintained multiple API versions simultaneously. This allowed different departments to migrate to the new version at their own pace, preventing system-wide disruption. Their version management strategy included clear deprecation policies and migration guides for API consumers.

3.1.3 Integration Patterns

Integration patterns in modern HRIS form the backbone of seamless data flow across the organization. These patterns determine how different systems communicate, share data, and maintain consistency across the enterprise landscape.

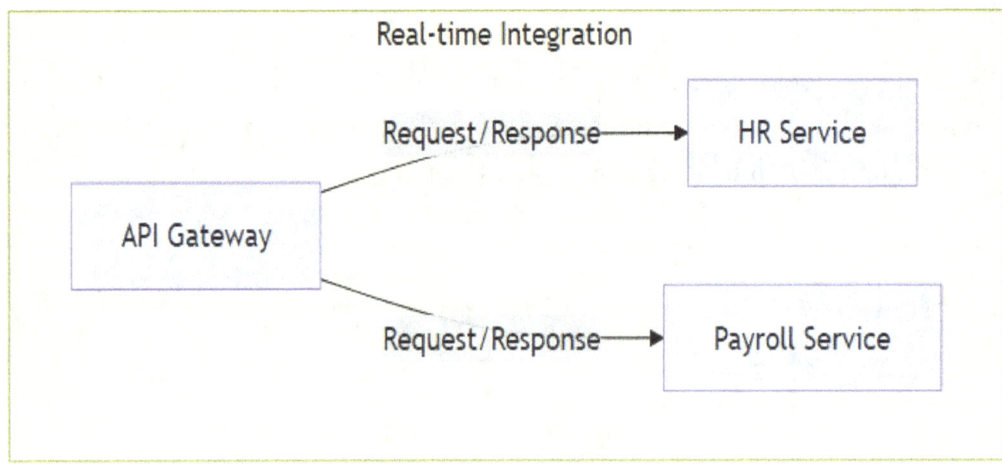

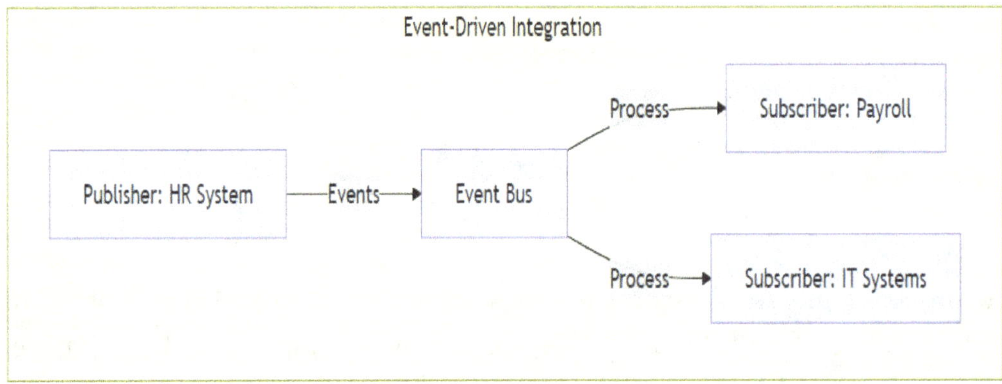

Event-driven integration has transformed how HRIS systems handle complex workflows. When MegaCorp implemented this pattern, they saw dramatic improvements in their onboarding process. Instead of rigid, synchronous processes, they created an event stream that different departments could subscribe to. When HR initiates onboarding, the event triggers automatic actions across IT, facilities, and training departments. This decoupled approach increased efficiency while reducing coordination overhead.

Real-time integration patterns become crucial for time-sensitive operations. Consider payroll processing, where accuracy and timeliness are non-negotiable. Modern HRIS implementations use synchronous APIs with circuit breakers and fallback mechanisms. When the payroll service requests attendance data, the system must ensure immediate consistency. Companies like PayRight Solutions implement sophisticated retry mechanisms and data validation checks to maintain data integrity during these critical operations.

Data synchronization patterns vary based on business needs. Some organizations implement Change Data Capture (CDC) patterns to track and propagate data changes across systems. Others use bulk synchronization for less time-critical data. The key is choosing the right pattern for each integration scenario. For instance, employee benefit elections might use eventual consistency, while tax withholding changes require immediate synchronization.

Integration security patterns have evolved to meet modern threats. Zero-trust architecture principles guide how systems authenticate and authorize each other. Every service-to-service communication is authenticated, encrypted, and authorized, regardless of network location. This approach has become particularly crucial with the rise of cloud-based HRIS solutions and remote work environments.

The modern HRIS architecture combines these patterns to create robust, scalable, and maintainable systems that can adapt to changing business needs while maintaining data integrity and system performance. As organizations continue to evolve, these architectural patterns provide the flexibility and resilience needed to support the future of HR operations.

In our next chapter, we'll explore how these architectural patterns translate into practical implementation strategies, examining real-world case studies and best practices for building modern HRIS solutions.

3.2 Data Architecture

The foundation of any robust HRIS lies in its data architecture. While modern architectural patterns provide the framework for system interactions, data architecture determines how organizations store, manage, and leverage their most valuable asset – employee data. A well-designed data architecture not only ensures data integrity and accessibility but also enables strategic HR initiatives and analytics-driven decision-making.

3.2.1 Employee Data Model

The employee data model serves as the digital representation of an organization's workforce. Unlike traditional flat data structures, modern employee data models are sophisticated, hierarchical, and dynamic, reflecting the complex nature of contemporary employment relationships.

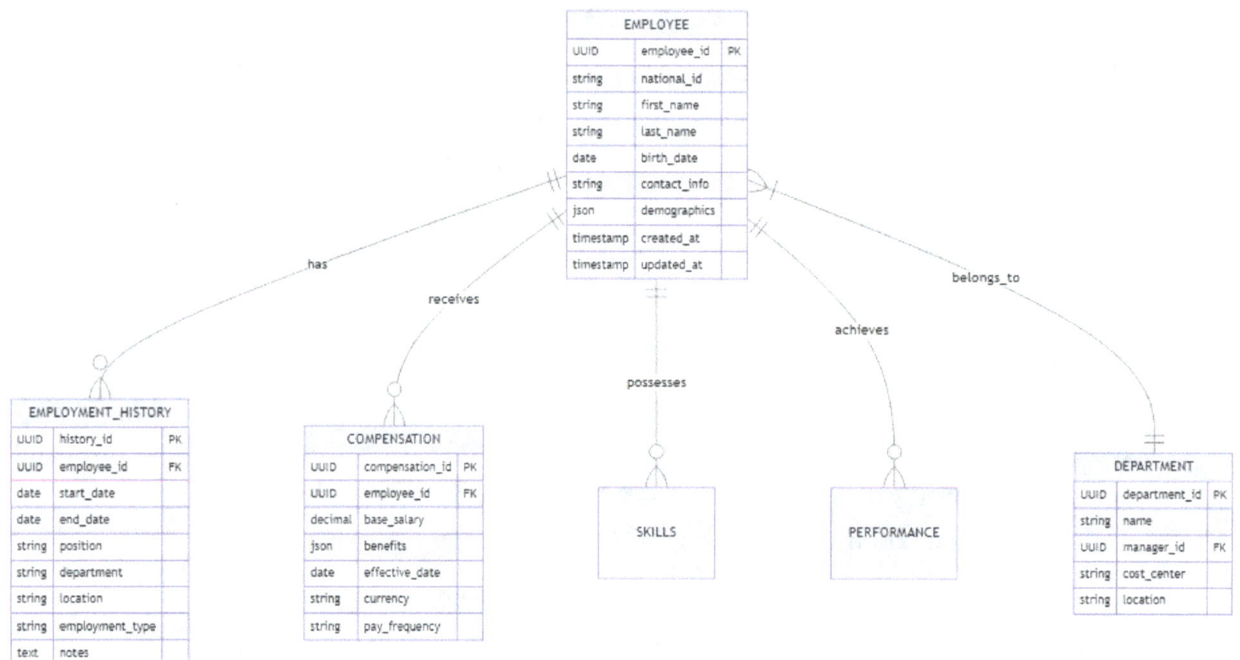

Consider how Global Dynamics revolutionized their employee data model when expanding internationally. Their previous model struggled with varying employment regulations and compensation structures across countries. The new model introduced a flexible schema that accommodates different employment types, compensation packages, and regulatory requirements while maintaining data consistency.

The modern employee data model extends beyond basic biographical information. It captures the dynamic nature of employment relationships through temporal data modeling. For instance, when tracking an employee's career progression, we need to maintain not just their current position but their entire employment history. This historical data becomes crucial for succession planning, compliance reporting, and workforce analytics.

Let's examine the key components of a sophisticated employee data model:

1. Core Identity Management

At the heart of the model lies the employee's core identity. Modern implementations use Universal Unique Identifiers (UUIDs) rather than sequential numbers, facilitating data integration across systems and preventing identifier conflicts during mergers or system migrations. TechCorp learned this lesson during a merger when they discovered both companies used the same employee ID format, leading to potential conflicts. Their solution involved implementing a UUID-based system with additional metadata to maintain legacy ID references.

2. Temporal Data Handling

Employment data is inherently temporal. Consider compensation history: we need to track not just current salary but all historical changes, including the reasons for changes and their effective dates. Modern data models implement temporal tables or bitemporal modeling to maintain this historical information accurately.

3. Hierarchical Relationships

Modern organizations have complex reporting structures that change frequently. The data model must capture these relationships while maintaining historical accuracy. When FastTrack Industries implemented their new data model, they used closure tables to efficiently manage hierarchical relationships, enabling quick access to both direct and indirect reporting relationships.

4. Flexible Attribution

Different regions and departments often require custom employee attributes. Rather than creating new columns for each attribute, modern data models implement flexible attribute stores using JSON or JSONB data types. This approach provides the flexibility to add new attributes without schema changes while maintaining query performance through appropriate indexing strategies.

3.2.2 Master Data Management

Master Data Management (MDM) in HRIS contexts goes beyond simple data governance – it's about ensuring that employee data remains consistent, accurate, and accessible across all organizational systems while maintaining compliance with increasingly complex privacy regulations.

Global First Bank's journey to implement MDM illustrates common challenges and solutions. They struggled with employee data inconsistencies across their HRIS, payroll, and learning management systems. Their MDM implementation established a "golden record" for each employee while maintaining system-specific attributes in connected applications.

Key aspects of modern MDM implementation include:

1. Data Governance Framework

Successful MDM requires a robust governance framework. This isn't just about technology – it's about establishing clear policies and procedures for data management. MegaCorp implemented a data stewardship program where designated individuals in each department were responsible for maintaining data quality within their domain. They used workflow automation to enforce data governance policies while maintaining efficiency.

2. Data Quality Management

Modern MDM systems employ sophisticated data quality rules. These rules go beyond simple validation to include complex business logic. For instance, when an employee transfers departments, the system checks not just the validity of the new department code but also ensures compliance with organizational policies, updates security access, and triggers necessary workflow approvals.

3. Entity Resolution and Matching

In large organizations, identifying and merging duplicate records becomes crucial. Advanced MDM systems use machine learning algorithms for entity resolution. TechGlobal's MDM system employs probabilistic matching algorithms that consider multiple attributes to identify potential duplicates, even when data contains variations or errors.

4. Temporal Data Management

Modern MDM systems must maintain historical accuracy while supporting current operations. This involves sophisticated versioning strategies and temporal data management. Consider how FastTrack Solutions implemented bitemporal data management in their MDM system, allowing them to track both the actual timing of events and when the data was known to the system – crucial for accurate audit trails and compliance reporting.

5. Privacy and Compliance

With regulations like GDPR and CCPA, MDM systems must incorporate privacy by design. This includes features like:

- Data minimization through automatic archiving

- Consent management tracking

- Right to be forgotten implementation

- Data residency compliance

Global Corp's MDM implementation includes sophisticated data classification and retention policies. Their system automatically identifies and manages sensitive data elements, applying appropriate security controls and retention policies based on data classification and jurisdictional requirements.

The success of MDM initiatives often depends on change management and user adoption. When MegaTech implemented their MDM solution, they created a comprehensive training program and established clear communication channels for data quality issues. Their approach included regular data quality metrics reporting and incentives for departments maintaining high data quality standards.

Modern MDM systems also incorporate API-first design principles, making master data services available through well-documented APIs. This enables seamless integration with both internal systems and external partners while maintaining data governance controls. The APIs include sophisticated validation rules and business logic, ensuring that all data changes adhere to established governance policies regardless of the source system.

Chapter 3: HRIS Solution Architecture (continued)

3.2 Data Architecture

3.2.3 Data Security & Privacy

In today's digital landscape, securing employee data isn't just about compliance – it's about maintaining trust and protecting one of an organization's most sensitive assets. Modern HRIS data security architecture must address evolving threats while ensuring data remains accessible to authorized users and systems.

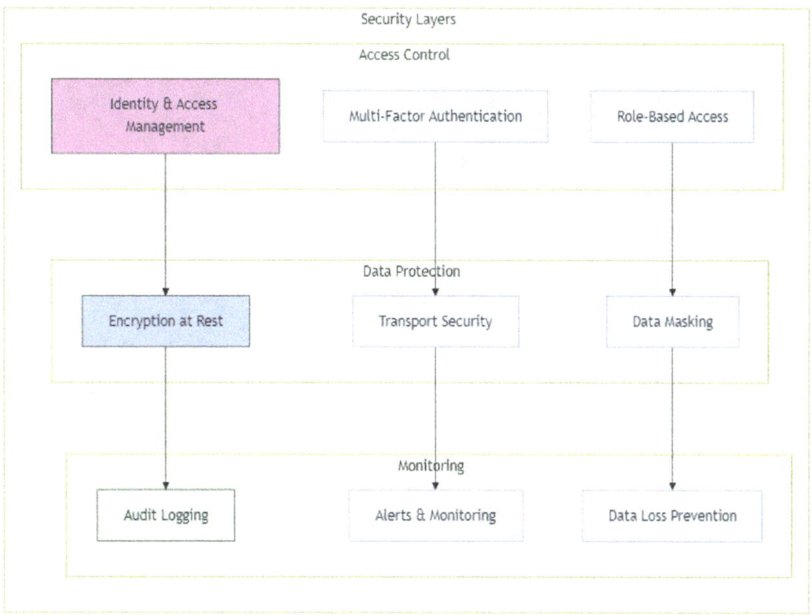

Implementing comprehensive data security requires a multi-layered approach. Global Financial Services transformed their HRIS security architecture after a security assessment revealed potential vulnerabilities. Their journey illustrates the essential components of modern HRIS data security:

1. Identity and Access Management (IAM)

Modern HRIS implementations require sophisticated IAM solutions that go beyond simple username/password authentication. Consider how TechCorp implemented their IAM strategy:

- Unified Identity Management

They implemented Single Sign-On (SSO) across all HR applications while maintaining granular access controls. The system uses SAML 2.0 for authentication, allowing seamless integration with their corporate identity provider while maintaining detailed audit trails of all access attempts.

- Contextual Access Control

Access decisions consider multiple factors:

```json
{
  "access_policy": {
    "user_attributes": {
      "role": "HR_Manager",
      "department": "HR",
      "location": "US"
    },
    "resource_attributes": {
      "data_classification": "Sensitive",
      "data_jurisdiction": "EU"
    },
    "context_attributes": {
      "time_of_day": "working_hours",
      "device_trust_level": "managed",
      "network_location": "corporate"
    }
  }
}
```

2. Data Protection Mechanisms

Data protection in HRIS requires multiple layers of security controls:

- Encryption at Rest

All sensitive employee data is encrypted using industry-standard algorithms. MegaCorp implements transparent data encryption (TDE) with regular key rotation:

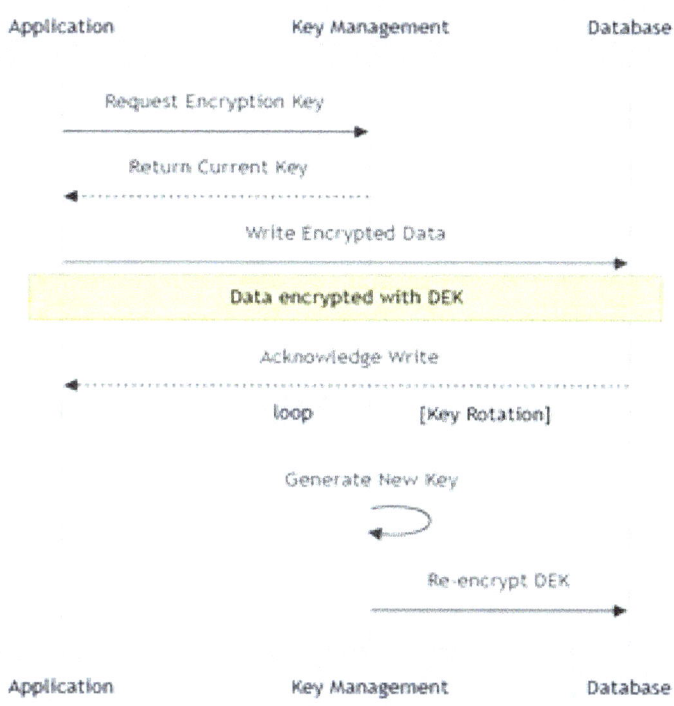

- Data Masking and Tokenization

Different user roles see different levels of data detail. For example, when accessing employee salary information:

- HR managers see full details

- Department managers see salary bands

- Team leads see only relative compensation levels

3. Privacy Management

Modern privacy requirements demand sophisticated controls:

- Data Residency Management

Global organizations must navigate complex data residency requirements. FastTrack Industries implemented a distributed data architecture that maintains employee data in appropriate geographical regions while ensuring global HR operations continue smoothly.

- Consent Management

The system maintains detailed records of employee privacy preferences and consent:

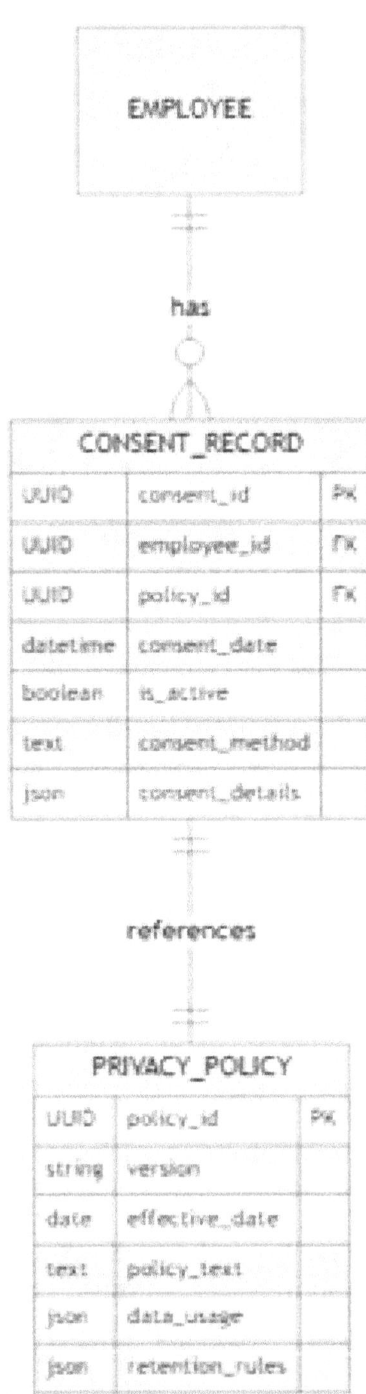

4. Audit and Monitoring

Comprehensive audit trails are crucial for security and compliance:

- Activity Monitoring

The system logs all data access and modifications:

```json
json
{
  "audit_event": {
    "timestamp": "2024-03-15T14:30:00Z",
    "user_id": "john.doe@company.com",
    "action": "VIEW_SALARY",
    "resource_id": "EMP123",
    "access_context": {
      "ip_address": "10.0.0.1",
      "device_id": "LAPTOP-123",
      "location": "New York Office"
    },
    "data_accessed": {
      "fields": ["current_salary", "effective_date"],
      "purpose": "Annual Review"
    }
  }
}
```

- Anomaly Detection

Modern HRIS implementations use machine learning to detect unusual patterns of data access or modification. TechGlobal's system automatically flags suspicious activities like:

- Unusual volumes of record access

- Access patterns outside normal working hours

- Unexpected changes to sensitive fields

5. Incident Response

A robust incident response framework is essential:

- Data Breach Response

The system includes automated procedures for potential data breaches:

1. Immediate access suspension for suspicious accounts

2. Automatic notification to security teams

3. Evidence preservation for investigation

4. Structured communication workflows for stakeholder notification

6. Compliance Management

Modern HRIS security architecture must address various compliance requirements:

- Regulatory Compliance

The system maintains compliance with multiple frameworks:

- GDPR for European operations

- CCPA for California employees

- PDPA for Asian operations

- Industry-specific regulations

- Compliance Monitoring

Automated compliance checks ensure ongoing adherence to security policies:

```json
{
  "compliance_check": {
    "policy_id": "SEC-001",
    "check_type": "DATA_RETENTION",
    "parameters": {
      "retention_period": "7_years",
      "data_type": "payroll_records"
    },
    "last_check": "2024-03-15T00:00:00Z",
    "status": "compliant",
    "actions_required": []
  }
}
```

The implementation of robust data security and privacy measures requires ongoing attention and evolution. Organizations must regularly assess their security posture, update their controls, and adapt to new threats and regulatory requirements. Success in this area comes from treating security not as a one-time project but as an integral part of the HRIS architecture that evolves with the organization's needs and the changing threat landscape.

3.3 AI/ML Components Integration

The integration of Artificial Intelligence and Machine Learning into HRIS represents a paradigm shift in how organizations manage their human capital. These technologies transform raw HR data into actionable insights, automate routine tasks, and provide predictive capabilities that were previously impossible.

3.3.1 Predictive Analytics

Predictive analytics in HRIS moves HR decision-making from reactive to proactive by leveraging historical data to forecast future trends and outcomes. This capability has become increasingly crucial for strategic workforce planning and risk management.

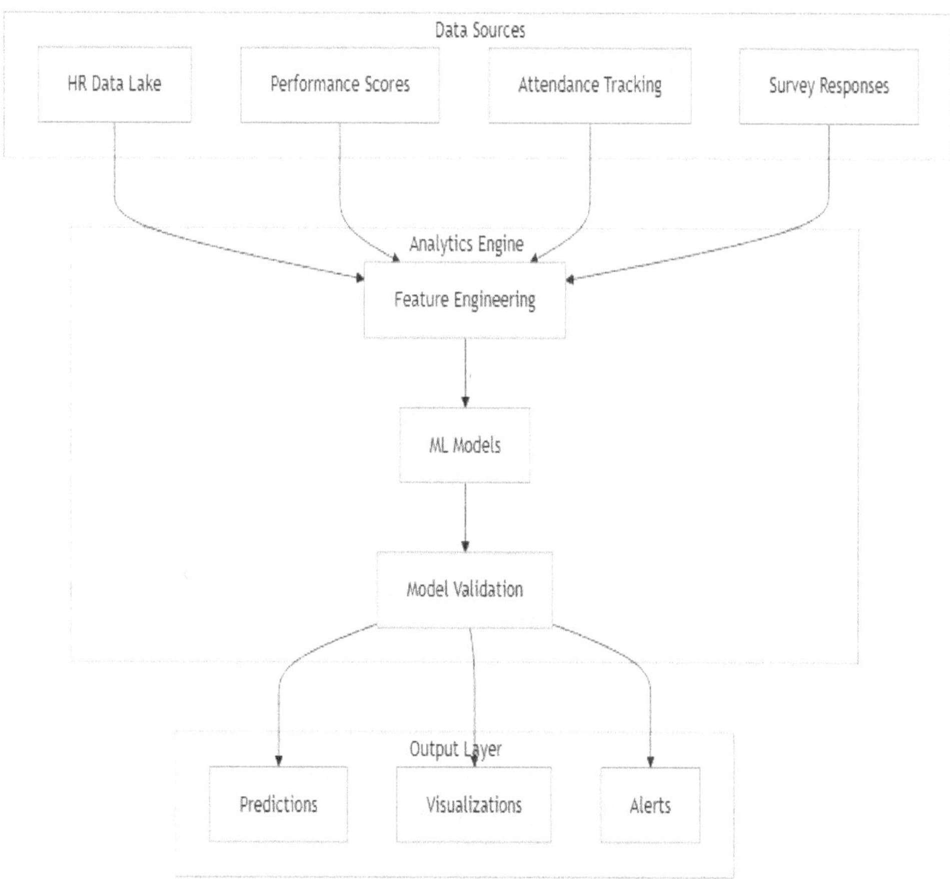

Consider how TechGlobal revolutionized their retention management using predictive analytics. Their system analyzes various data points to predict employee flight risk:

```python
# Example Feature Set for Retention Prediction
retention_features = {
    "performance_metrics": [
        "last_review_score",
        "trend_over_past_reviews",
        "project_completion_rate"
    ],
    "engagement_indicators": [
        "survey_participation",
        "internal_network_activity",
        "learning_platform_usage"
    ],
    "work_patterns": [
        "overtime_hours",
        "vacation_usage",
        "meeting_attendance"
    ]
}
```

The system implements sophisticated machine learning models:

1. Employee Attrition Prediction

- Uses gradient boosting algorithms

- Incorporates temporal features

- Provides probability scores with confidence intervals

2. Career Path Modeling

The system analyzes successful career trajectories to suggest optimal development paths:

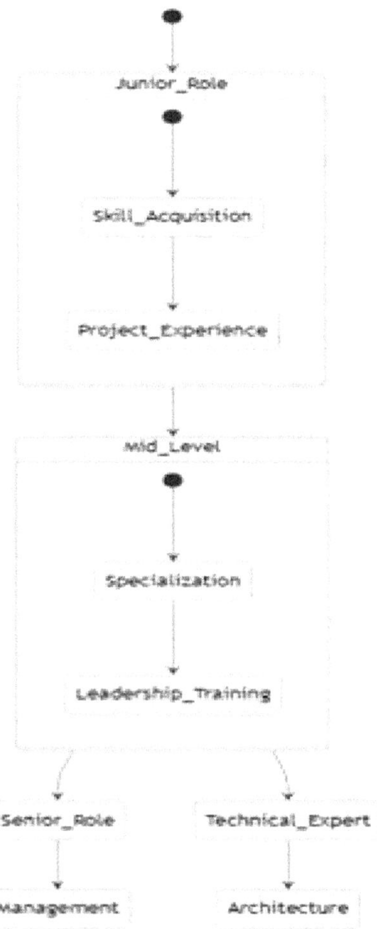

3.3.2 Automated Workflows

AI-powered workflow automation transforms traditional HR processes into intelligent, adaptive systems that can handle complex scenarios with minimal human intervention.

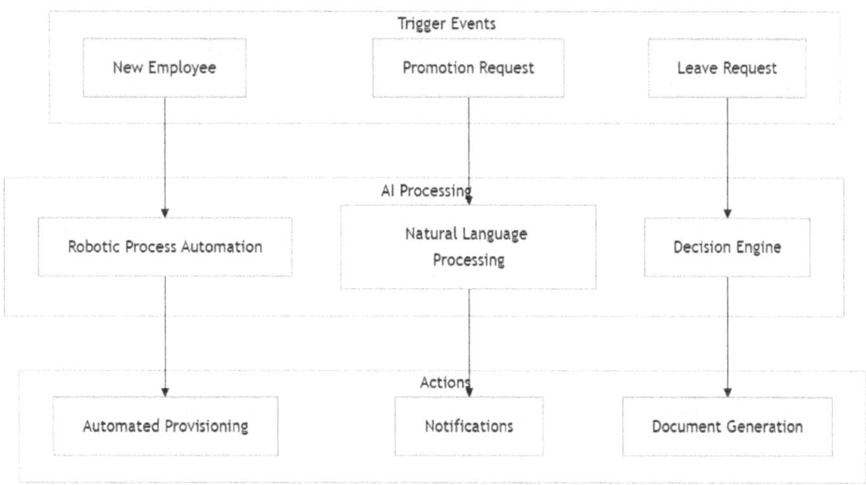

MegaCorp implemented intelligent workflows for their onboarding process:

1. Document Processing

The system uses Natural Language Processing (NLP) to:

- Extract information from resumes and documents

- Validate data against existing records

- Generate personalized onboarding documents

```json
{
  "document_processor": {
    "input_type": "resume",
    "extraction_fields": {
      "personal_info": {
        "confidence_threshold": 0.95,
        "required_fields": ["name", "contact", "education"]
      },
      "experience": {
        "pattern_matching": true,
        "temporal_analysis": true
      }
    },
    "validation_rules": {
      "cross_reference": "existing_employee_database",
      "format_verification": "standard_templates"
    }
  }
}
```

2. Intelligent Routing

The system learns from historical patterns to optimize workflow routing:

python

class WorkflowRouter:

```
    def determine_path(self, request_type, context):
        # Consider multiple factors for routing
        factors = {
            "request_urgency": self.calculate_urgency(context),
            "approver_workload": self.get_approver_metrics(),
            "historical_patterns": self.analyze_past_flows(),
            "compliance_requirements":
self.check_compliance_needs(request_type)
        }


        return self.ml_model.predict_optimal_path(factors)
```

3.3.3 Intelligent Reporting

Modern HRIS platforms leverage AI to transform traditional reporting into dynamic, insight-driven analytics that adapt to user needs and organizational context.

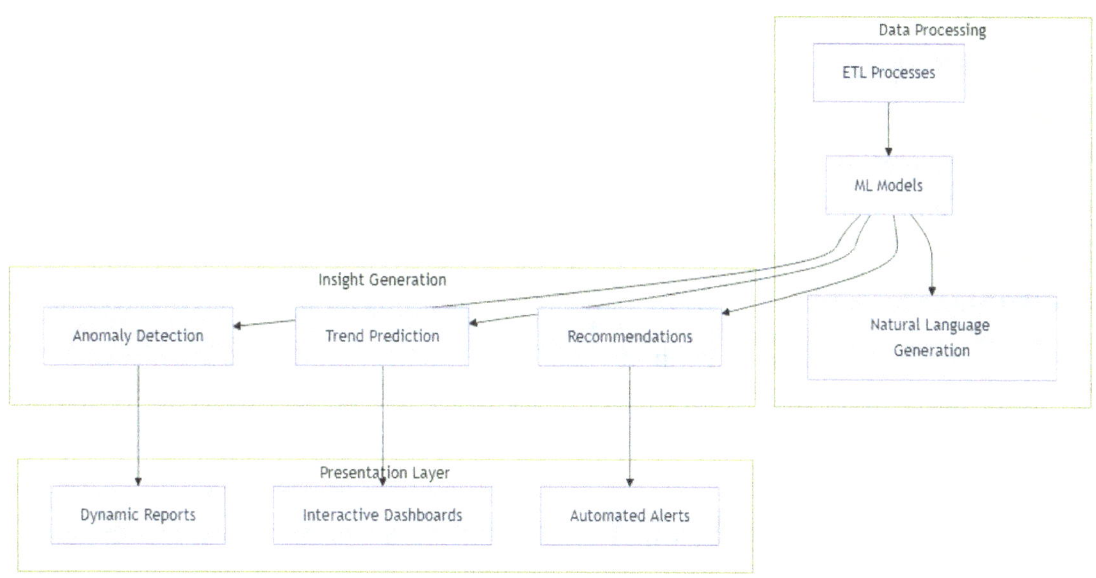

FastTrack Solutions implemented intelligent reporting with several innovative features:

1. Natural Language Generation

The system generates narrative insights from data:

python

```python
def generate_insight_narrative(data_point, context):
    narrative_template = {
        "turnover_spike": {
            "pattern": "Observed {percent_increase}% increase in turnover in {department}, significantly above the historical average of {historical_avg}%",
            "recommendations": [
                "Review recent organizational changes",
                "Conduct focused stay interviews",
                "Analyze compensation competitiveness"
            ]
        }
    }

    return NarrativeGenerator.create(
        template=narrative_template,
        data=data_point,
        context=context
    )
```

2. Adaptive Dashboards

The system learns from user interaction patterns:

- Automatically highlights relevant metrics

- Suggests new visualization types

- Personalized data presentation based on role and preferences

3. Predictive Reporting

Reports include forward-looking insights:

- Workforce planning projections

- Budget forecasting

- Skill gap analysis

```json
{
  "predictive_report": {
    "timeframe": "Q3_2024",
    "predictions": {
      "headcount_needs": {
        "engineering": "+15",
        "sales": "+8",
        "confidence_level": 0.85
      },
      "budget_impact": {
        "additional_cost": "$1.2M",
        "roi_timeline": "9_months"
      }
    },
    "action_items": [
      {
        "type": "recruitment_planning",
        "priority": "high",
        "timeline": "start_immediately"
      },
      {
        "type": "budget_adjustment",
        "priority": "medium",
        "timeline": "next_quarter"
      }
    ]
  }
}
```

The integration of AI/ML components into HRIS architecture requires careful consideration of:

- Data Quality: Ensuring input data meets the quality requirements for ML models

- Model Governance: Establishing frameworks for model validation and monitoring

- Ethical AI: Implementing safeguards against bias and ensuring fair outcomes

- Integration Architecture: Creating seamless connections between AI components and existing systems

Organizations must also consider the change management aspects of AI integration:

- User Training: Helping users understand and trust AI-generated insights

- Process Adaptation: Modifying existing processes to leverage AI capabilities

- Continuous Improvement: Establishing feedback loops for model refinement

The successful integration of AI/ML components transforms HRIS from a record-keeping system into a strategic tool that provides actionable insights and automates complex workflows. This evolution continues as new AI capabilities emerge and organizations find innovative ways to apply them to HR challenges.

3.4 Security & Compliance

In today's digital landscape, securing HRIS data while maintaining compliance with ever-evolving regulations presents a complex challenge. Modern HRIS architectures must implement robust security measures while ensuring system accessibility and regulatory adherence.

3.4.1 Identity Management

Modern identity management in HRIS extends far beyond simple username and password combinations. It encompasses the entire lifecycle of digital identities within an organization, from creation to retirement.

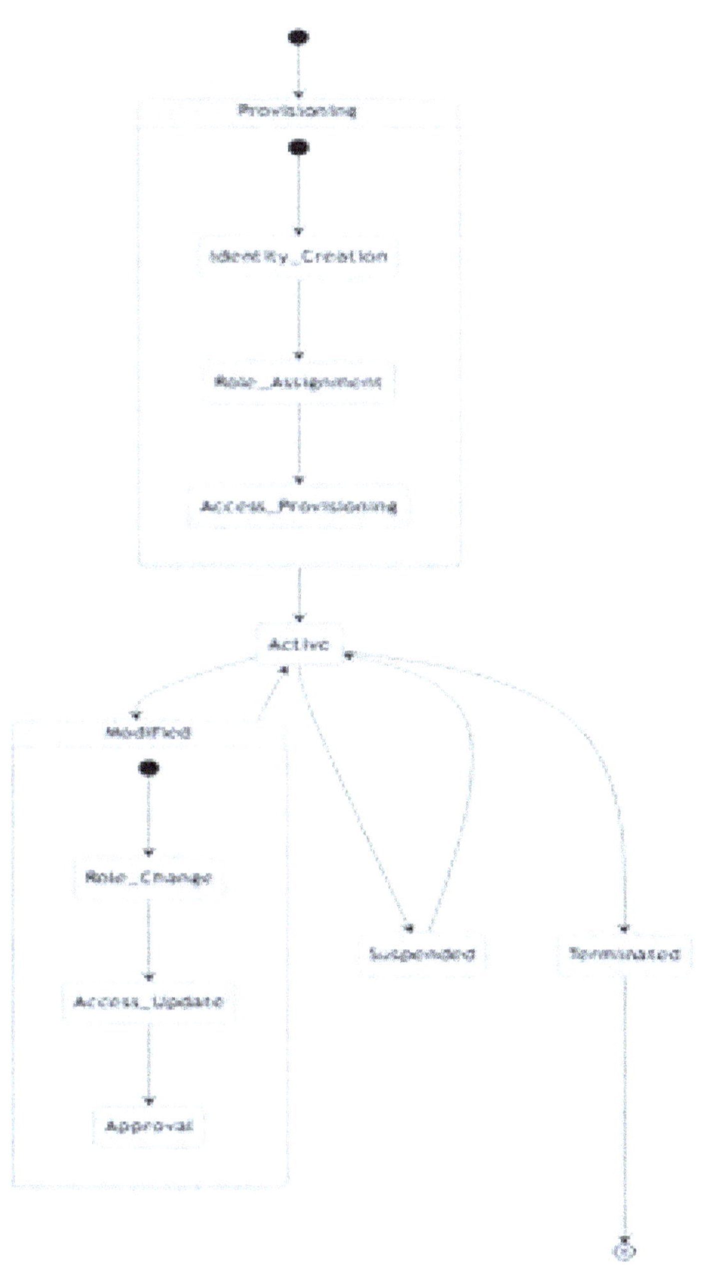

Provisioning
Identity_Creation
Role_Assignment
Access_Provisioning
Active
Modified
Role_Change
Access_Update
Approval
Suspended
Terminated

Let's examine how Global Financial implemented their identity management system:

1. Identity Lifecycle Management

```json
{
  "identity_profile": {
    "user_id": "jsmith_2024",
    "identity_type": "employee",
    "lifecycle_state": {
      "current_stage": "active",
      "previous_stages": [
        {
          "stage": "provisioning",
          "timestamp": "2024-01-15T09:00:00Z",
          "approver": "hr_admin"
        }
      ],
      "scheduled_changes": {
        "role_change": {
          "effective_date": "2024-04-01",
          "new_role": "senior_analyst",
          "approval_chain": ["direct_manager", "hr_manager"]
        }
      }
    }
  }
}
```

2. Authentication Infrastructure

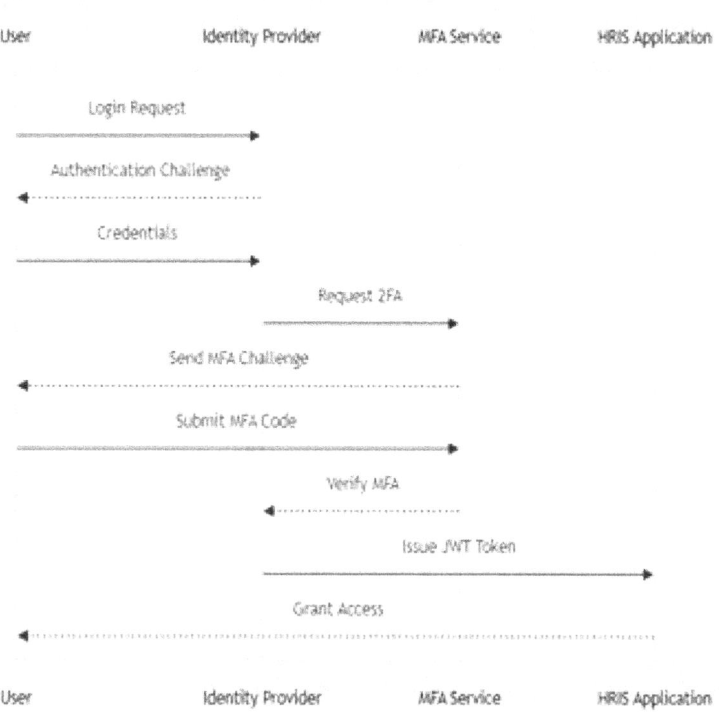

3. Federation and Single Sign-On

TechCorp implemented enterprise-wide SSO with sophisticated session management:

python

```python
class SessionManager:
    def create_session(self, user_context):
        session = {
            "session_id": generate_uuid(),
            "authentication": {
                "method": "sso",
                "provider": "corporate_idp",
                "security_context": {
                    "ip_address": user_context.ip,
                    "device_fingerprint": user_context.device_id,
                    "risk_score": calculate_risk_score(user_context)
                }
```

```
    },
    "permissions": derive_permissions(user_context.roles),
    "session_policies": {
        "max_duration": "8_hours",
        "idle_timeout": "30_minutes",
        "require_step_up": ["salary_view", "termination_process"]
    }
}
return session
```

3.4.2 Access Control

Modern HRIS access control implements a sophisticated, multi-layered approach that goes beyond traditional role-based access control (RBAC).

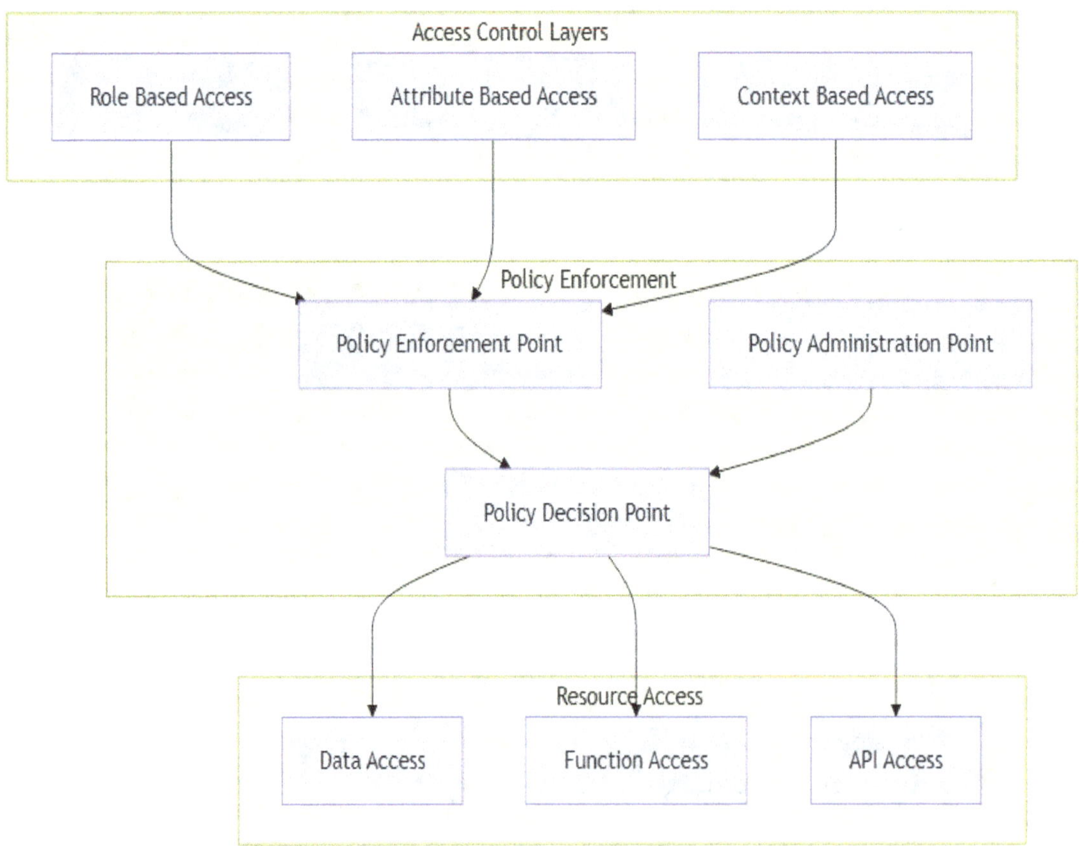

1. Attribute-Based Access Control (ABAC)

MegaCorp implemented sophisticated ABAC policies:

python

```python
def evaluate_access(request, context):
    policy = {
        "subject_attributes": {
            "role": context.user.role,
            "department": context.user.department,
            "clearance_level": context.user.clearance
        },
        "resource_attributes": {
            "classification": request.resource.classification,
            "owner_department": request.resource.department,
            "sensitivity_level": request.resource.sensitivity
        },
        "environmental_attributes": {
            "time": context.current_time,
            "location": context.access_location,
            "device_trust_level": context.device.trust_level
        }
    }

    return AccessEvaluator.evaluate(policy, request)
```

2. Dynamic Access Control

FastTrack Solutions implemented context-aware access control:

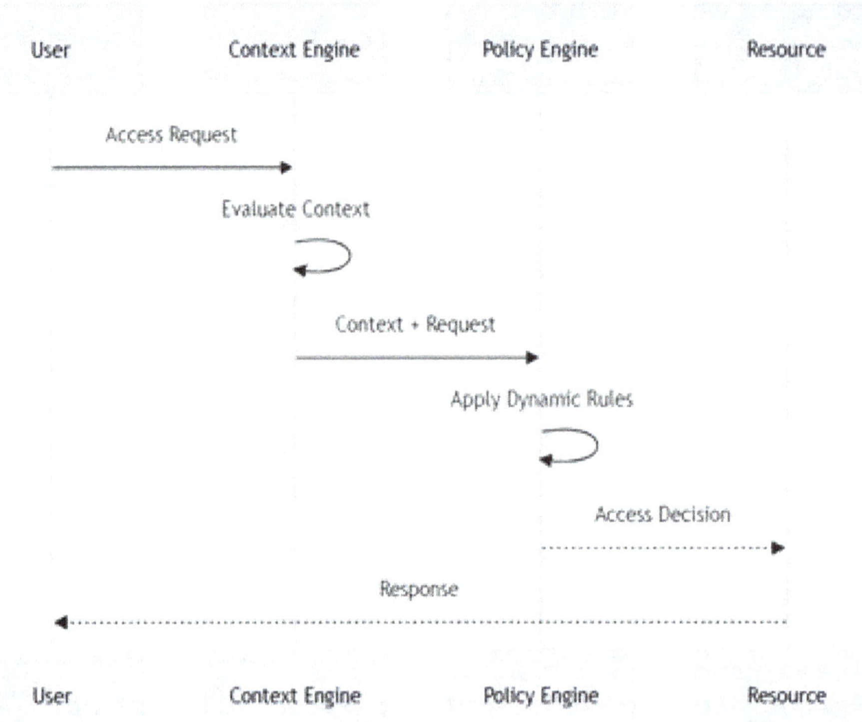

3.4.3 Compliance Requirements

Modern HRIS must navigate a complex landscape of regulatory requirements while maintaining operational efficiency.

1. Regulatory Framework Integration

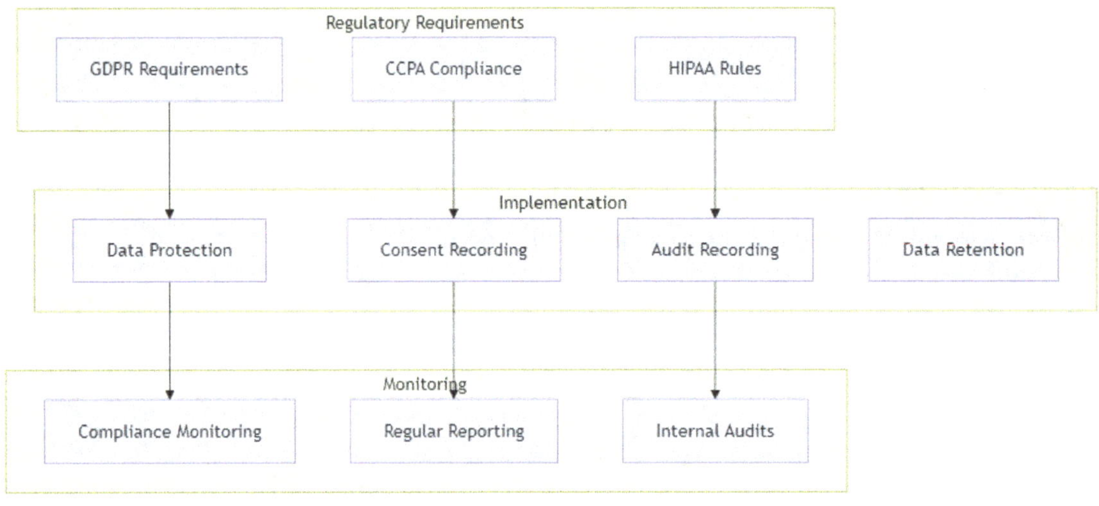

2. Data Privacy Implementation

python

```python
class PrivacyManager:
    def handle_data_request(self, request_type, user_id):
        privacy_actions = {
            "access_request": self.provide_data_copy,
            "deletion_request": self.execute_deletion,
            "correction_request": self.process_correction,
            "restriction_request": self.apply_restrictions
        }

        return privacy_actions[request_type](user_id)


    def execute_deletion(self, user_id):
        deletion_plan = {
            "immediate_deletion": [
                "contact_details",
                "performance_reviews"
            ],
            "scheduled_deletion": {
                "payroll_records": "7_years",
                "tax_documents": "5_years"
            },
            "permanent_records": [
                "employment_dates",
                "position_history"
            ]
        }
        return self.process_deletion_plan(deletion_plan)
```

3. Audit Trail Implementation

GlobalCorp's comprehensive audit system:

```json
{
  "audit_record": {
    "event_id": "evt_20240315_123456",
    "timestamp": "2024-03-15T14:30:00Z",
    "actor": {
      "user_id": "admin_jane",
      "role": "hr_manager",
      "department": "human_resources"
    },
    "action": {
      "type": "data_access",
      "resource": "employee_salary",
      "operation": "view",
      "target_id": "emp_789"
    },
    "context": {
      "location": "headquarters",
      "device": "registered_laptop_123",
      "network": "corporate_vpn"
    },
    "compliance_metadata": {
      "retention_period": "7_years",
      "classification": "sensitive",
      "legal_basis": "legitimate_business_purpose"
    }
  }
}
```

4. Regulatory Reporting

Automated compliance reporting system:

python

class ComplianceReporter:

```python
    def generate_report(self, regulation_type, time_period):

        metrics = {

            "data_access_requests": self.count_access_requests(),

            "consent_changes": self.track_consent_updates(),

            "data_deletions": self.monitor_deletions(),

            "security_incidents": self.collect_incidents(),

            "response_times": self.calculate_response_metrics()

        }


        return self.format_compliance_report(metrics)
```

The implementation of security and compliance in modern HRIS requires a balanced approach that ensures both protection and usability. Organizations must continuously update their security measures and compliance procedures to address new threats and regulatory requirements while maintaining system efficiency and user experience.

Regular security assessments, compliance audits, and user training programs are essential components of a comprehensive security and compliance strategy. The key is to build security and compliance into the system architecture from the ground up, rather than treating them as add-on features.

3.5 Performance & Scalability

In modern HRIS architectures, performance and scalability are not afterthoughts but fundamental design considerations that directly impact user satisfaction and system effectiveness. As organizations grow and user demands increase, the ability to maintain consistent performance while scaling efficiently becomes crucial.

3.5.1 System Performance Optimization

Performance optimization in HRIS requires a holistic approach that addresses multiple layers of the application stack and considers various usage patterns unique to HR operations.

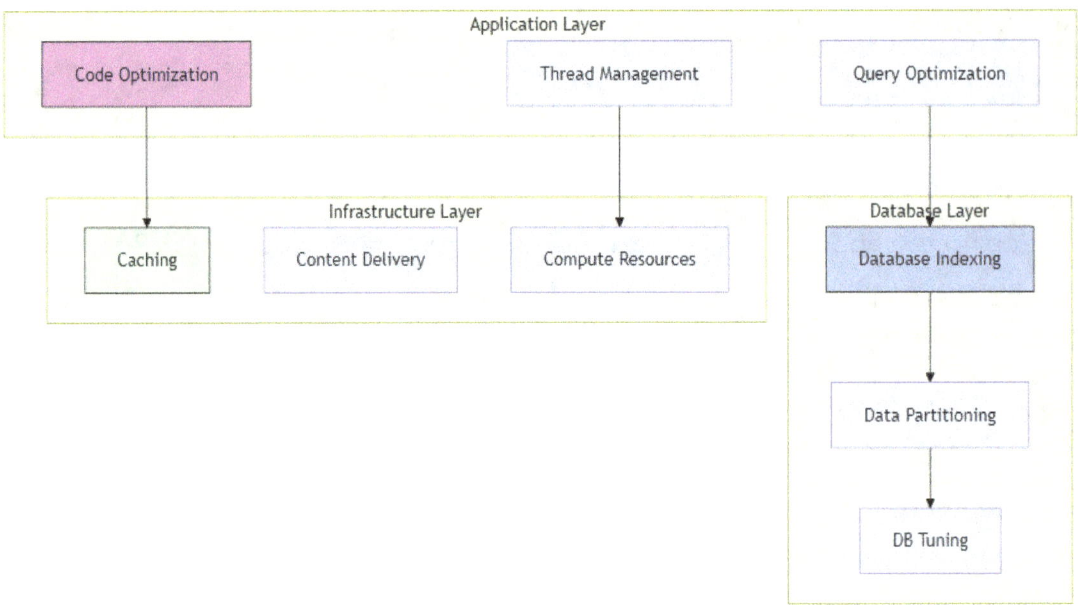

Let's examine how TechGlobal optimized their HRIS performance:

1. Database Optimization

They implemented sophisticated query optimization strategies:

sql

– Example of optimized employee search query

```sql
WITH employee_hierarchy AS (
    SELECT
        e.employee_id,
        e.manager_id,
        array_agg(d.department_name) OVER (
            PARTITION BY e.department_id
        ) as dept_hierarchy
    FROM employees e
    JOIN departments d ON e.department_id = d.department_id
    WHERE e.status = 'ACTIVE'
)
SELECT /*+ INDEX(employees emp_name_idx) */
```

```sql
    e.employee_id,
    e.first_name,
    e.last_name,
    eh.dept_hierarchy
FROM employees e
JOIN employee_hierarchy eh ON e.employee_id = eh.employee_id
WHERE e.last_updated_date > :last_sync_date
```

2. Application-Level Optimization

Performance profiling revealed critical paths:

python

```python
class PerformanceOptimizer:
    def optimize_bulk_operations(self, operation_type):
        optimization_strategies = {
            "payroll_processing": {
                "batch_size": 1000,
                "parallel_threads": 4,
                "priority_queue": True
            },
            "report_generation": {
                "async_processing": True,
                "caching_strategy": "time_based",
                "cache_ttl": 3600
            }
        }

        return self.apply_optimization(
            operation_type,
            optimization_strategies[operation_type]
        )
```

3.5.2 Load Balancing & High Availability

Modern HRIS systems must maintain high availability while handling variable loads, particularly during peak periods like benefits enrollment or performance review cycles.

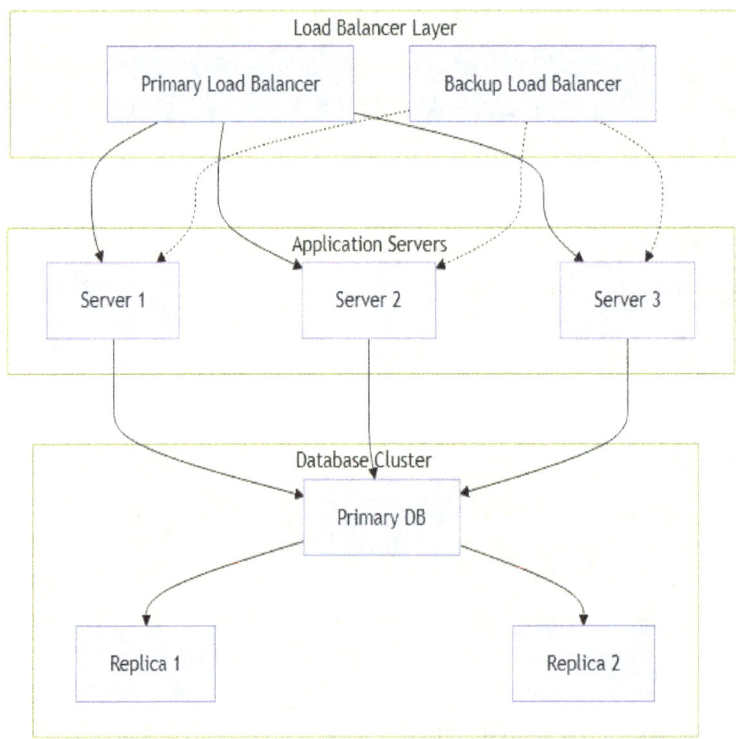

MegaCorp implemented sophisticated load balancing:

1. Dynamic Load Distribution

python

class LoadBalancer:

```python
    def distribute_load(self, request, server_pool):
        server_metrics = {
            server.id: {
                "current_load": self.get_server_load(server),
                "response_time": self.get_avg_response_time(server),
                "health_score": self.calculate_health_score(server),
                "geographic_location": server.location
            }
            for server in server_pool
        }

        return self.select_optimal_server(server_metrics, request)
```

2. Failover Management

```json
{
  "failover_config": {
    "monitoring": {
      "health_check_interval": "15s",
      "failure_threshold": 3,
      "success_threshold": 2
    },
    "failover_rules": {
      "automatic_failover": true,
      "fallback_priority": [
        "same_region",
        "nearest_region",
        "any_available"
      ],
      "data_sync_requirements": {
        "max_lag_tolerance": "5s",
        "sync_priority": "high"
      }
    }
  }
}
```

3.5.3 Caching Strategies

Effective caching is crucial for HRIS performance, especially for frequently accessed data and compute-intensive operations.

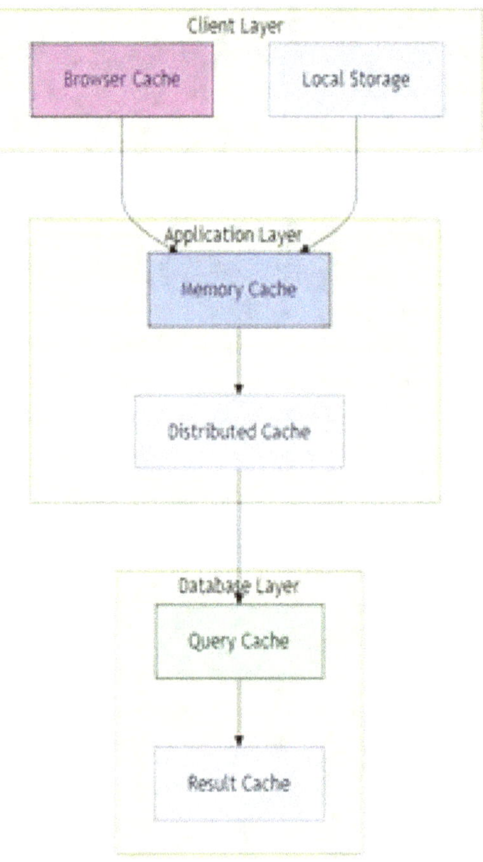

FastTrack Solutions implemented a comprehensive caching strategy:

1. Multi-Level Caching

python

```python
class CacheManager:
    def get_cached_data(self, key, context):
        cache_hierarchy = {
            "l1_cache": {
                "type": "memory",
                "ttl": 300,  # 5 minutes
                "strategy": "lru"
            },
            "l2_cache": {
                "type": "redis",
                "ttl": 3600,  # 1 hour
```

```python
        "strategy": "write_through"
    },
    "l3_cache": {
        "type": "cdn",
        "ttl": 86400,  # 24 hours
        "strategy": "stale_while_revalidate"
    }
}


return self.fetch_from_cache_hierarchy(
    key,
    cache_hierarchy,
    context
)
```

2. Intelligent Cache Invalidation

python

```python
class CacheInvalidator:
    def invalidate_cache(self, event):
        invalidation_rules = {
            "employee_update": {
                "patterns": [
                    "employee:{id}",
                    "department:{dept_id}:employees",
                    "org_chart:*"
                ],
                "priority": "high"
            },
            "payroll_run": {
                "patterns": [
                    "payroll:summary:*",
                    "employee:{id}:compensation"
                ],
```

```python
        "priority": "critical"
        }
    }

    return self.process_invalidation(
        event,
        invalidation_rules
    )
```

3. Cache Warming Strategies

```python
python
class CacheWarmer:
    def warm_cache(self, scenario):
        warming_strategies = {
            "system_startup": {
                "priority_data": [
                    "company_policies",
                    "department_structures",
                    "common_lookup_values"
                ],
                "load_order": "parallel",
                "precompute_views": True
            },
            "daily_refresh": {
                "priority_data": [
                    "active_employees",
                    "current_payroll_period",
                    "pending_approvals"
                ],
                "load_order": "sequential",
                "precompute_views": False
            }
        }
```

```
        return self.execute_warming_strategy(
            scenario,
            warming_strategies[scenario]
        )
```

Performance and scalability in modern HRIS require continuous monitoring and optimization. Organizations must:

1. Implement robust monitoring systems to track performance metrics

2. Regularly review and optimize database queries and application code

3. Maintain effective caching strategies that balance freshness with performance

4. Ensure high availability through proper load balancing and failover mechanisms

5. Plan for scalability based on organizational growth and usage patterns

The key to success lies in treating performance and scalability as ongoing concerns rather than one-time optimization efforts. Regular performance audits, load testing, and capacity planning help ensure that the HRIS continues to meet organizational needs as they evolve.

Chapter 3: HRIS Solution Architecture (continued)

Best Practices and Case Studies

Best Practices Implementation

Building upon our earlier discussions, let's explore proven best practices that successful organizations have implemented in their HRIS architectures.

```mermaid
graph TB
    subgraph "Architecture Principles"
        SC[Scalable Design]
        HA[High Availability]
        SEC[Security First]
        INT[Integration Ready]
```

```
    end

    subgraph "Implementation Guidelines"
        MON[Monitoring]
        TEST[Testing Strategy]
        DOC[Documentation]
        GOV[Governance]
    end

    subgraph "Operational Excellence"
        SLA[SLA Management]
        INC[Incident Response]
        CHG[Change Management]
        PER[Performance Tuning]
    end

    SC --> MON
    HA --> TEST
    SEC --> DOC
    INT --> GOV

    MON --> SLA
    TEST --> INC
    DOC --> CHG
    GOV --> PER


```

1. Architecture Design Best Practices

python

```python
class ArchitectureValidator:
    def validate_design_principles(self, architecture_component):
        validation_rules = {
            "scalability": {
                "horizontal_scaling": True,
                "stateless_design": True,
                "data_partitioning": True
            },
            "reliability": {
                "fault_tolerance": True,
                "data_redundancy": True,
                "disaster_recovery": True
            },
            "security": {
                "zero_trust": True,
                "encryption_at_rest": True,
                "encryption_in_transit": True
            }
        }
        return self.perform_validation(
            architecture_component,
            validation_rules
        )
```

Case Study 1: Global Financial Services Transformation

Let's examine how Global Financial Services (GFS) transformed their HRIS architecture to support 50,000 employees across 30 countries.

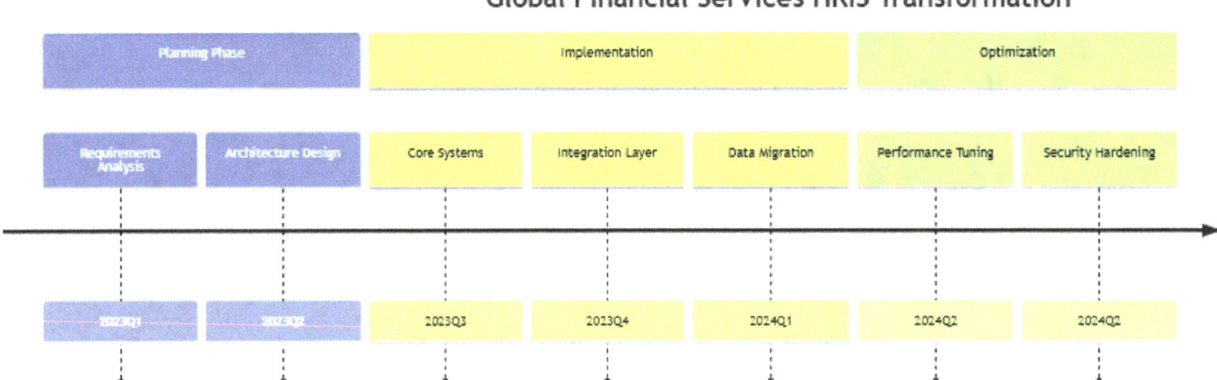

Key Challenges and Solutions:

json

```json
{
  "transformation_challenges": {
    "data_migration": {
      "challenge": "Legacy systems with inconsistent data formats",
      "solution": {
        "approach": "Phased migration with data cleansing",
        "tools": ["ETL pipeline", "Data validation framework"],
        "metrics": {
          "data_quality_improvement": "87%",
          "migration_success_rate": "99.99%"
        }
      }
    },
```

```
    "global_compliance": {
      "challenge": "Multiple regulatory frameworks",
      "solution": {
        "approach": "Region-specific data handling",
        "implementation": {
          "data_residency": "Multi-region deployment",
          "privacy_controls": "Granular access policies"
        }
      }
    }
  }
}
```

Results:

- 40% reduction in processing time

- 99.99% system availability

- 60% decrease in compliance-related incidents

Case Study 2: TechCorp's Performance Optimization

TechCorp faced significant performance challenges during peak HR operations. Here's how they resolved them:

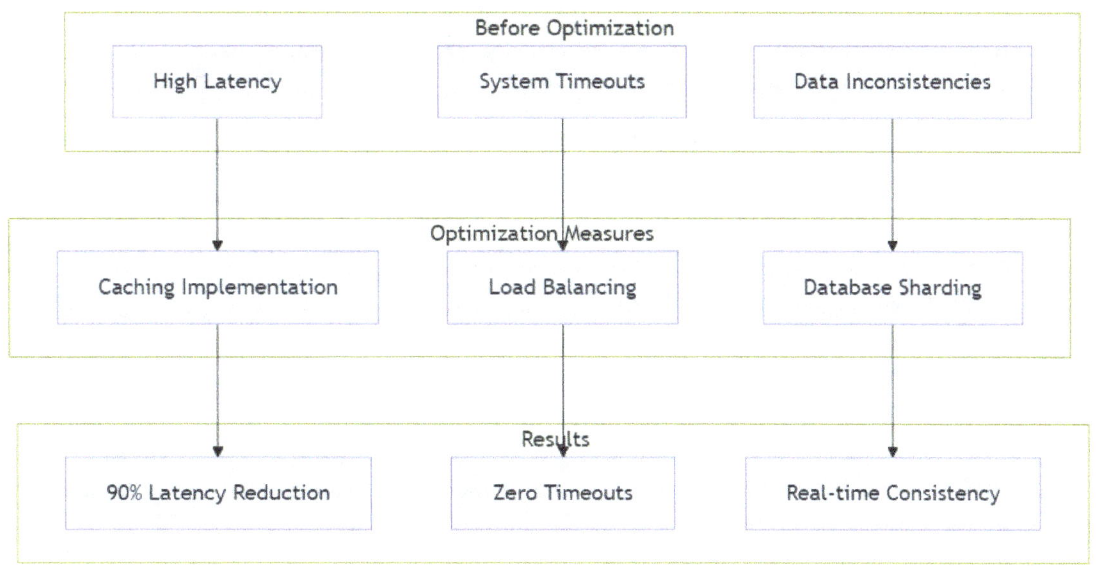

Implementation Details:

python

```python
class PerformanceOptimizationCase:
    def document_optimization_strategy(self):
        return {
            "caching_strategy": {
                "implementation": "Multi-layer caching",
                "technologies": ["Redis", "CDN", "Browser Cache"],
                "results": {
                    "response_time_improvement": "90%",
                    "cache_hit_ratio": "95%"
                }
            },
            "load_balancing": {
                "approach": "Dynamic load distribution",
                "metrics": {
                    "server_utilization": "75%",
                    "request_distribution": "Even"
                }
            },
            "database_optimization": {
                "sharding_strategy": "Geographic",
                "query_optimization": "Automated",
                "performance_gain": "85%"
            }
        }
```

Case Study 3: FastTrack Solutions' Integration Success

FastTrack Solutions successfully integrated multiple HR systems across their global operations.

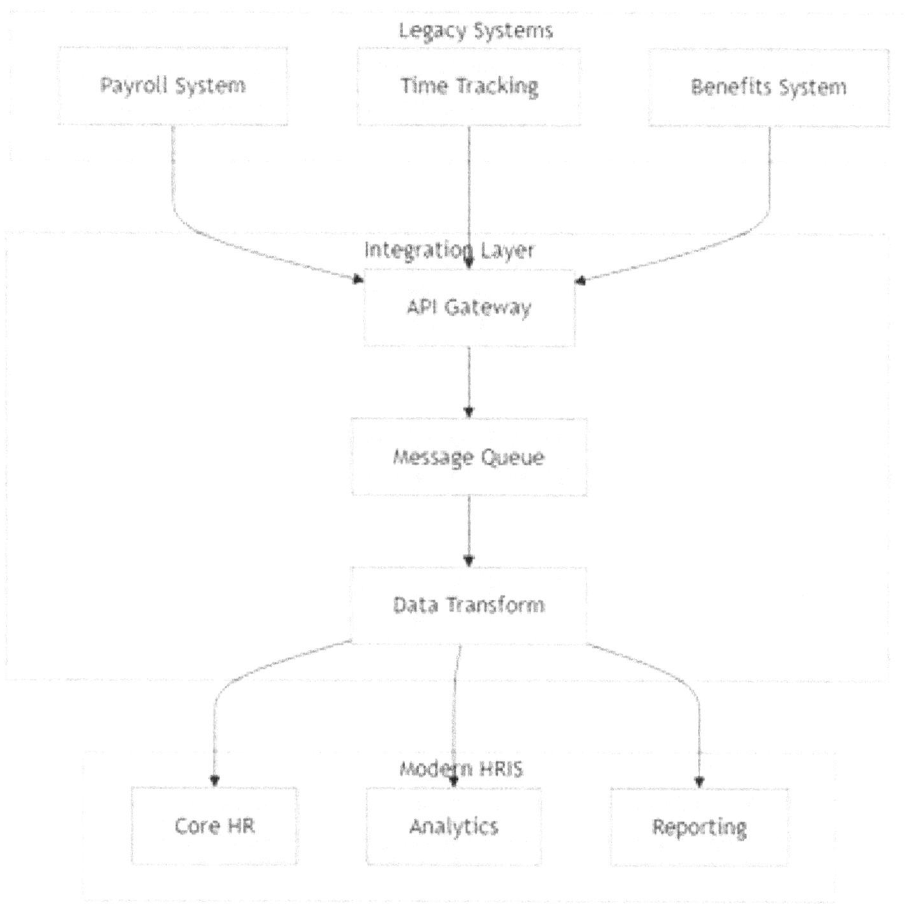

Integration Metrics:

```json
json
{
  "integration_metrics": {
    "system_connectivity": {
      "uptime": "99.99%",
      "response_time": "<100ms",
      "error_rate": "<0.01%"
    },
    "data_synchronization": {
      "real_time_sync": "95%",
      "batch_processing": "5%",
```

```
      "data_accuracy": "99.99%"
    },
    "business_impact": {
      "process_automation": "85%",
      "manual_intervention": "reduced_by_90%",
      "reporting_efficiency": "improved_by_75%"
    }
  }
}
```

Key Lessons Learned

1. Planning and Strategy

- Comprehensive requirements gathering is crucial

- Stakeholder involvement at all stages

- Phased implementation approach

2. Technical Considerations

- Build for scale from the start

- Implement robust monitoring

- Regular performance optimization

3. Change Management

- User training is critical

- Clear communication strategy

- Feedback loops for continuous improvement

Future Considerations

As HRIS architecture continues to evolve, organizations should prepare for:

1. Emerging Technologies

- AI/ML integration

- Blockchain for credential verification

- Advanced analytics capabilities

2. Changing Workforce Needs

- Remote work support

- Global compliance requirements

- Enhanced security measures

3. Integration Capabilities

- API-first design

- Real-time data synchronization

- Extended ecosystem integration

These best practices and case studies demonstrate that successful HRIS implementation requires a balanced approach combining technical excellence with strategic business alignment. Organizations must remain flexible and adaptable while maintaining focus on core requirements and user needs.

Chapter 4
HRIS Implementation & Deployment

Implementing and deploying a Human Resource Information System (HRIS) is a transformative initiative that can redefine how organizations manage their human resources. This chapter delves into the core pillars of implementation, addressing the strategic, technical, and cultural dimensions critical to success. By focusing on a phased approach, migration planning, and change management, organizations can navigate the complexities of HRIS deployment effectively while building a foundation for future growth.

4.1 Implementation Strategy

A well-structured implementation strategy is the backbone of a successful HRIS deployment. This strategy should balance business priorities, technical feasibility, and user adoption. Without a strategic framework, even the most advanced HRIS systems can fail to deliver the expected value. The following sections explore critical aspects of the implementation strategy, providing actionable insights and real-world examples.

4.1.1 Phased Approach

A phased approach breaks the HRIS deployment into smaller, manageable segments, each focusing on specific functionalities or user groups. This method mitigates risk, optimizes resource allocation, and provides opportunities for iterative improvement.

Initial Deployment: Organizations often begin with core HR modules, such as employee records, organizational hierarchies, and payroll. By focusing on foundational processes, they ensure that critical functions are operational before introducing more complex modules like performance management or advanced analytics.

Gradual Scaling: Once the initial modules stabilize, the rollout can expand to cover additional functionalities. For example, after deploying payroll in the first phase, the second phase might focus on benefits administration, ensuring that users have time to adapt to one system component before transitioning to the next.

Iterative Learning: A phased approach also enables organizations to incorporate lessons learned during earlier phases into subsequent stages. For instance, if feedback from early users highlights the need for a more intuitive interface, adjustments can be made before the next phase. This flexibility is especially beneficial for large-scale or multi-geography rollouts where local regulations or practices may differ.

Scenarios for Future Architecture: The phased approach aligns seamlessly with modular and API-based architectures. In the future, organizations can introduce advanced capabilities, such as machine learning-driven talent analytics or chatbots for employee self-service, as separate modules without overhauling the entire system.

Example: A global manufacturing company started its HRIS deployment in one country before expanding to its international offices. By resolving localization issues and adapting to regulatory requirements in the initial region, the company saved significant time and resources when scaling globally.

Challenges: While the phased approach minimizes risks, it requires meticulous planning to ensure continuity between phases. Interdependencies between modules must be identified early to avoid integration issues, such as payroll depending on unimplemented time-tracking modules.

4.1.2 Migration Planning

Migration planning is the linchpin that ensures a seamless transition from legacy systems to the new HRIS. It involves a comprehensive process to move data, streamline workflows, and maintain data integrity, which is critical to organizational trust in the new system.

Data Cleansing and Validation: Migration planning begins with data cleansing to eliminate outdated, redundant, or erroneous information. For example, outdated employee records or incorrect payroll details can lead to cascading errors in the new system. Data validation ensures that only accurate and relevant data is transferred, reducing the risk of future discrepancies.

Mapping Data Fields: Mapping involves correlating fields in the legacy system to the corresponding fields in the HRIS. For instance, a legacy system may store employee identification numbers differently than the HRIS, requiring transformation during migration. This step ensures that critical data such as tax details, employment history, and benefits enrollment are accurately reflected in the new system.

Mock Migrations and Testing: Mock migrations simulate the data transfer process in a sandbox environment, allowing teams to identify and resolve issues without disrupting business operations. This step is particularly important for complex HRIS implementations, where inaccuracies could affect employee payroll or compliance reporting.

Integration Challenges: Migrating data often requires bridging gaps between legacy systems and modern HRIS platforms. For example, older systems may use flat files, while HRIS systems leverage REST APIs. Employing middleware like MuleSoft or Informatica can facilitate this transition by acting as a conduit for data exchange.

Future Possibilities: Cloud-based data lakes can store historical data, enabling organizations to access legacy information without overloading the HRIS. Additionally, artificial intelligence (AI) tools can automate data cleansing and mapping, further streamlining migration processes.

Example: A healthcare organization migrating to a cloud-based HRIS faced challenges in consolidating records from multiple hospitals. By conducting mock migrations and utilizing ETL tools, they ensured a seamless transition that preserved data integrity and minimized disruption.

4.1.3 Change Management

Change management is essential for addressing the human aspect of HRIS deployment. While technical challenges are significant, the success of an HRIS implementation ultimately depends on how well employees and stakeholders adopt and use the system.

Cultural Shifts: An HRIS often requires employees to shift from manual or outdated systems to automated, data-driven workflows. This transition can create resistance among employees who may fear job displacement or feel overwhelmed by new technologies. A strong change management strategy addresses these concerns head-on, fostering a sense of inclusion and empowerment.

Stakeholder Engagement: Involving stakeholders early in the process is critical. Leadership teams must champion the HRIS initiative to build credibility and align organizational goals with implementation efforts. Additionally, creating cross-functional teams comprising HR professionals, IT experts, and end-users ensures diverse perspectives are considered.

Training Programs: Training is the linchpin of user adoption. Organizations should design tiered training programs tailored to different user roles. For example:

- HR managers may require in-depth training on reporting and analytics.
- Employees can focus on self-service functionalities like leave applications and benefits enrollment.
- IT teams may need advanced training to manage integrations and system configurations.

Feedback Mechanisms: Gathering feedback during and after deployment provides valuable insights into user experience. Surveys, focus groups, and user analytics help identify pain points and improve the system iteratively. For example, if employees report difficulty accessing certain features, additional training or system modifications can address these issues.

Sustaining Adoption: Post-implementation, organizations must continue to promote the system's benefits through regular updates, success stories, and feature showcases. For instance, highlighting how the HRIS improved recruitment efficiency or employee satisfaction reinforces its value to the organization.

Future Possibilities: Emerging technologies such as chatbots, virtual training platforms, and predictive analytics can enhance change management. A chatbot embedded in the HRIS could provide real-time guidance to employees, reducing the need for extensive training.

Example: A retail organization faced resistance from store managers during an HRIS rollout. By involving managers in pilot testing and addressing their concerns through targeted workshops, the company achieved a 90% adoption rate within six months.

An effective HRIS implementation strategy weaves together phased deployment, meticulous migration planning, and proactive change management. By addressing both technical and human challenges, organizations can ensure their HRIS not only meets immediate business needs but also evolves to support future goals. The insights and methodologies presented in this chapter provide a comprehensive roadmap for navigating the complexities of HRIS deployment, empowering organizations to transform their HR functions with confidence.

4.2 System Integration

The backbone of any modern HRIS implementation lies in its ability to seamlessly connect with other enterprise systems and data sources. System integration transforms an HRIS from a standalone application into a central hub of workforce management, enabling real-time data flow and process automation across the organization.

4.2.1 Third-party Integration

In today's HR technology landscape, organizations rarely rely on a single system to manage their entire HR operations. Third-party integrations extend HRIS capabilities by connecting with specialized solutions such as payroll processors, benefits administration platforms, learning management systems (LMS), and recruitment tools.

When implementing third-party integrations, several key considerations come into play:

API Integration Strategies Modern HRIS platforms typically offer robust APIs (Application Programming Interfaces) that facilitate communication with external systems. REST APIs have emerged as the industry standard, offering flexibility and scalability in integration design. For instance, when connecting an HRIS with an external payroll system, RESTful APIs enable real-time synchronization of employee data, ensuring accurate and timely payroll processing.

Authentication and Security Security cannot be an afterthought in third-party integrations. OAuth 2.0 has become the de facto standard for secure authentication, while API keys and JSON Web Tokens (JWT) provide additional layers of security. Consider a scenario where an HRIS connects with a benefits administration platform – secure authentication ensures that sensitive employee health information remains protected while enabling seamless benefits enrollment processes.

Data Synchronization Patterns Different integration scenarios demand different synchronization patterns. Real-time synchronization works well for critical updates like employee status changes, while batch processing might be more appropriate for less time-sensitive data like training records. A thoughtful synchronization strategy prevents system overload while maintaining data accuracy across platforms.

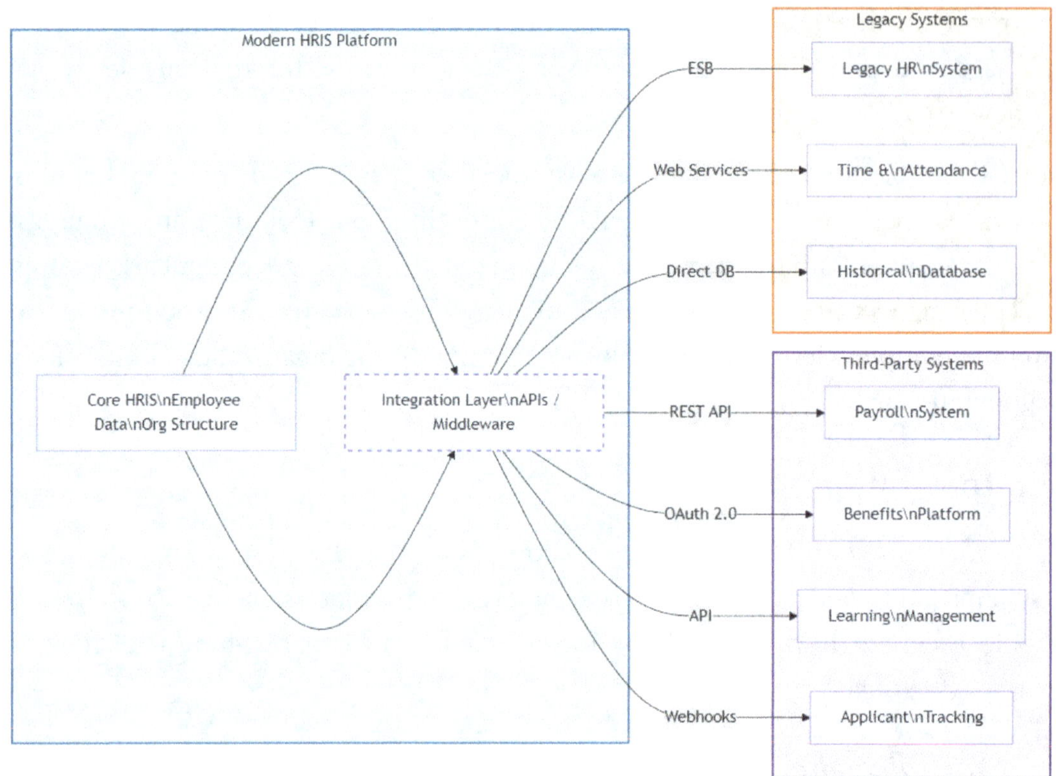

4.2.2 Legacy System Integration

Many organizations face the challenge of integrating modern HRIS solutions with existing legacy systems. These legacy systems often contain valuable historical data and support critical business processes, making their integration essential for operational continuity.

Integration Approaches Several strategies can bridge the gap between modern and legacy systems:

Middleware Solutions Enterprise Service Bus (ESB) or integration middleware can act as translators between modern and legacy systems. These solutions handle protocol conversion, data transformation, and message routing, enabling seamless communication between systems speaking different languages.

Web Services Wrapping Legacy systems can be "wrapped" with modern web service interfaces, creating an abstraction layer that makes them accessible to modern HRIS platforms. This approach minimizes changes to the legacy system while enabling modern integration capabilities.

Database-level Integration In some cases, direct database integration might be necessary, especially when dealing with legacy systems lacking modern APIs. While this approach requires careful handling to maintain data integrity, it can provide a practical solution for accessing historical data.

4.2.3 Data Migration

Data migration represents a critical phase in HRIS implementation, requiring careful planning and execution to ensure data accuracy and completeness in the new system.

Migration Strategy Development A successful data migration strategy encompasses several key elements:

Data Assessment and Cleaning Before migration begins, organizations must assess their existing data quality and address any inconsistencies. This might involve standardizing job titles, removing duplicate records, or updating outdated information. For example, an organization might discover multiple variations of the same job title (e.g., "Sr. Developer," "Senior Developer," "Sr Developer") that need standardization before migration.

Mapping and Transformation Creating detailed data mapping documents ensures that information from source systems correctly translates to the new HRIS. This includes handling different data formats, field lengths, and validation rules. Complex transformations might be necessary, such as splitting a single "name" field into separate "first name" and "last name" fields.

Validation and Testing Implementing robust validation procedures ensures data integrity throughout the migration process. This includes automated validation scripts and manual spot-checks of migrated data. Organizations should plan for multiple test migrations before the final cutover, with each iteration helping to refine the process and catch potential issues.

4.3 Deployment & Operations

Once the HRIS system has been configured and tested, it's time to deploy it into production and transition into ongoing operations. This phase focuses on standing up the live environment, optimizing performance, and establishing processes to keep the system running smoothly. Let's dive into the key aspects of deployment and operations.

4.3.1 Infrastructure Setup

Before the HRIS can be used by the organization, the underlying infrastructure needs to be put in place. This includes:

- **Server provisioning**: Allocating the necessary compute resources, whether on-premises or in the cloud, to run the HRIS application and databases. Considerations include CPU, memory, storage, and network bandwidth requirements.

- **Environment configuration**: Installing and configuring the operating systems, middleware, and dependencies required by the HRIS. This may involve deploying virtual machines, containers, or utilizing a platform-as-a-service model.

- **Security hardening**: Applying security best practices to lock down the infrastructure, such as enabling firewalls, closing unnecessary ports, and ensuring proper access controls and authentication mechanisms are in place.

- **High availability**: Designing the infrastructure for reliability and minimum downtime. Techniques like load balancing and data replication across multiple servers can help ensure the HRIS remains accessible even if individual components fail.

Here's a simplified diagram showing a potential HRIS deployment architecture:

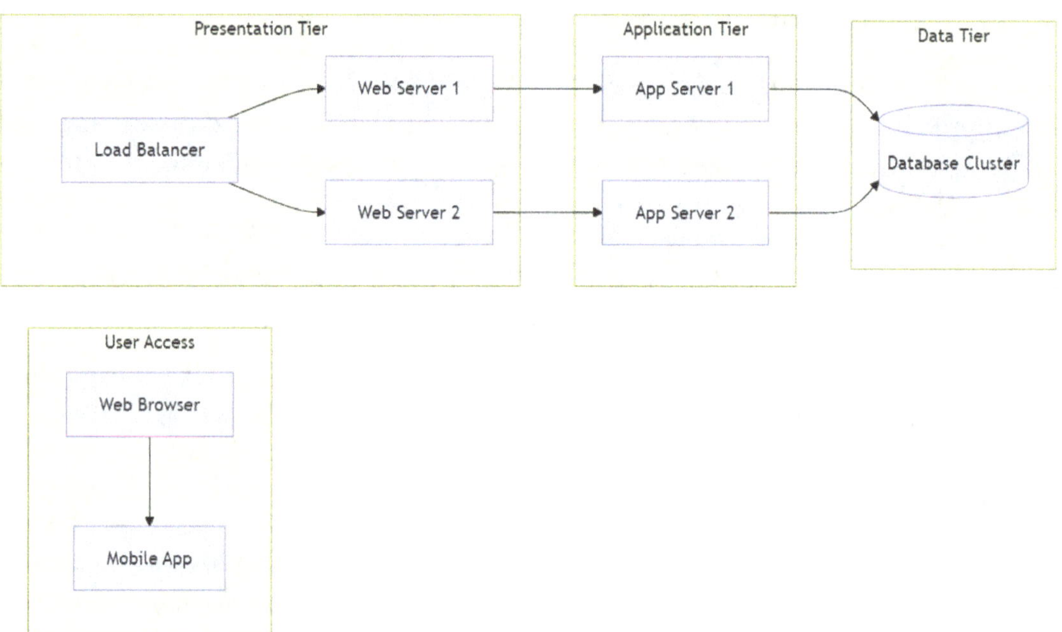

In this architecture, user requests come in through web browsers or a mobile app and hit a load balancer. The load balancer distributes the traffic between two web servers for high availability. The web servers render the user interface and pass requests to the application servers, which contain the core HRIS business logic. The app servers in turn interact with a clustered database to store and retrieve HR data in a persistent and fault-tolerant manner.

Of course, the actual architecture will depend on the specific HRIS platform and an organization's requirements. But this gives a general idea of the infrastructure components involved.

4.3.2 Performance Optimization

With the infrastructure in place, attention turns to making sure the HRIS delivers a responsive and snappy user experience. Some key performance optimization areas include:

- **Caching**: Implementing caching at various layers (web, application, database) to store frequently accessed data in memory and reduce repeated computation. Effective caching can dramatically improve response times.

- **Query optimization**: Analyzing and tuning database queries to minimize table scans, use efficient joins, and create appropriate indexes. Tools like query profilers and EXPLAIN plans help identify slow queries for optimization.

- **Asynchronous processing**: Offloading resource-intensive tasks to background worker processes so they don't block the main user interactions. For example, generating complex reports or running batch payroll jobs are good candidates for asynchronous processing.

- **Content distribution**: Serving static assets like images, stylesheets, and javascripts from a content delivery network (CDN) to reduce load on the main servers and deliver content from geographically closer locations to users.

- **Performance testing**: Conducting thorough performance tests with representative data and usage patterns to benchmark the system and identify bottlenecks. This should be done before go-live and periodically thereafter to ensure performance remains acceptable as data volumes grow.

4.3.3 Monitoring & Maintenance

Once live, the HRIS requires ongoing monitoring and maintenance to detect issues and keep it running optimally. Key practices include:

- **Proactive monitoring**: Setting up monitoring and alerting for key performance indicators, such as server resource utilization, application response times, error rates, and job failures. Monitoring tools can provide dashboards, notifications, and automated remediation workflows.

- **Capacity planning**: Tracking usage trends and projecting future growth to provision adequate compute, storage, and network resources in advance. Capacity planning prevents the HRIS from being overwhelmed by increasing data or user volumes.

- **Patch management**: Applying security patches and software updates in a timely manner to address vulnerabilities and take advantage of bug fixes and new features. Patches should be tested in non-production environments before being deployed to production.

- **Backups and disaster recovery**: Regularly backing up HRIS data and configuration and having a tested plan for recovering from disasters like data center outages, data corruption, or ransomware attacks. High availability and disaster recovery go hand in hand.

- **Support processes**: Documenting troubleshooting guides, FAQs, and escalation procedures to handle user inquiries and issues in a consistent and efficient manner. The HRIS team should have clearly defined roles and service level agreements (SLAs).

By proactively monitoring and maintaining the HRIS, organizations can minimize downtime and disruption to HR services. The goal is to catch and resolve issues before they impact users.

In this chapter, we explored the key aspects of HRIS deployment and ongoing operations. We discussed setting up the infrastructure, optimizing performance, and putting in place monitoring and maintenance processes.

The actual details will vary based on the specific HRIS platform and an organization's scale and needs. But the principles of high availability, performance optimization, and proactive maintenance apply universally.

Getting these elements right helps ensure the HRIS delivers a reliable and responsive experience to users and supports an organization's HR functions effectively. In the next chapter, we'll look at how to drive user adoption and realize the full benefits of the HRIS investment.

4.4 Post-Implementation

Congratulations, your new HRIS is now live! But the work doesn't stop there. In fact, the post-implementation phase is critical for realizing the full value of your HRIS investment. This is when you train users, support them through the transition, and continuously improve the system. Let's explore each of these areas in more detail.

4.4.1 User Training

One of the biggest factors in HRIS success is user adoption. You can have the most powerful, feature-rich system in the world, but if your users don't know how to use it effectively, you won't see the desired benefits. That's where training comes in.

Effective HRIS training needs to be:

- **Role-specific**: Users should be trained on the features and workflows that are relevant to their job duties. A benefits administrator needs different training than a hiring manager.

- **Hands-on**: Users learn best by doing. Training should involve actual system practice, not just lectures or demos. Consider a sandbox environment where users can experiment without fear of breaking anything.

- **Ongoing**: Training shouldn't be a one-and-done event. Provide refresher courses, training on new features, and resources for self-directed learning. As new hires join the organization, have a plan for onboarding them to the HRIS.

- **Measurable**: Track training completion rates and assess user competency through quizzes, surveys, or observation. Use this data to identify areas for improvement.

Here's an example of a phased HRIS training plan:

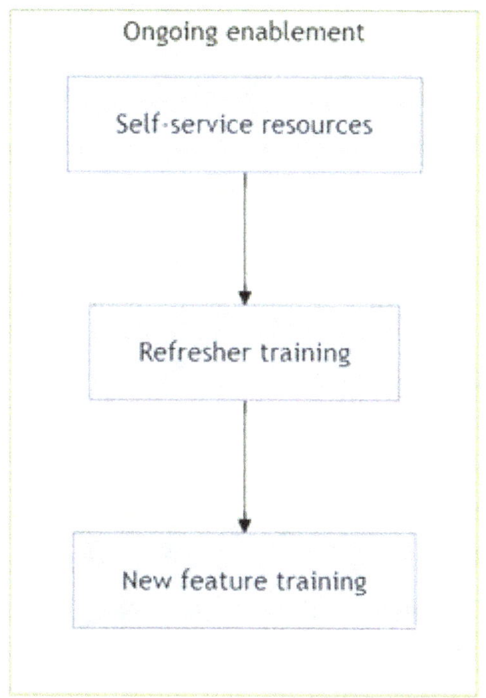

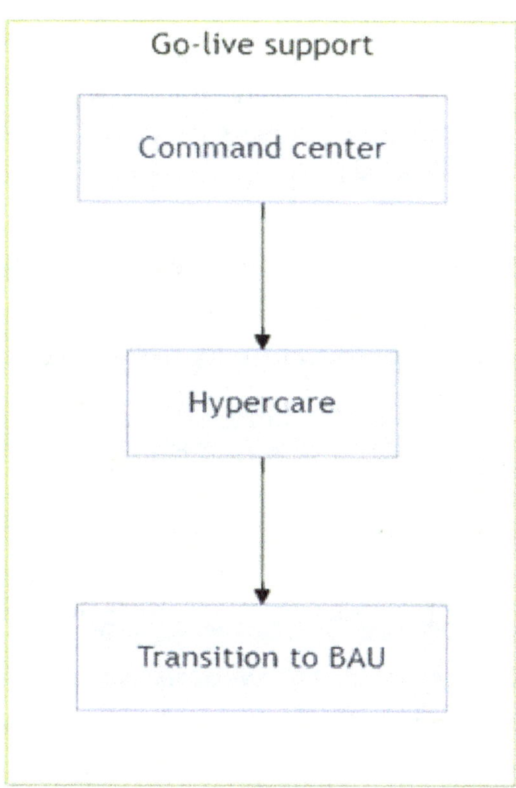

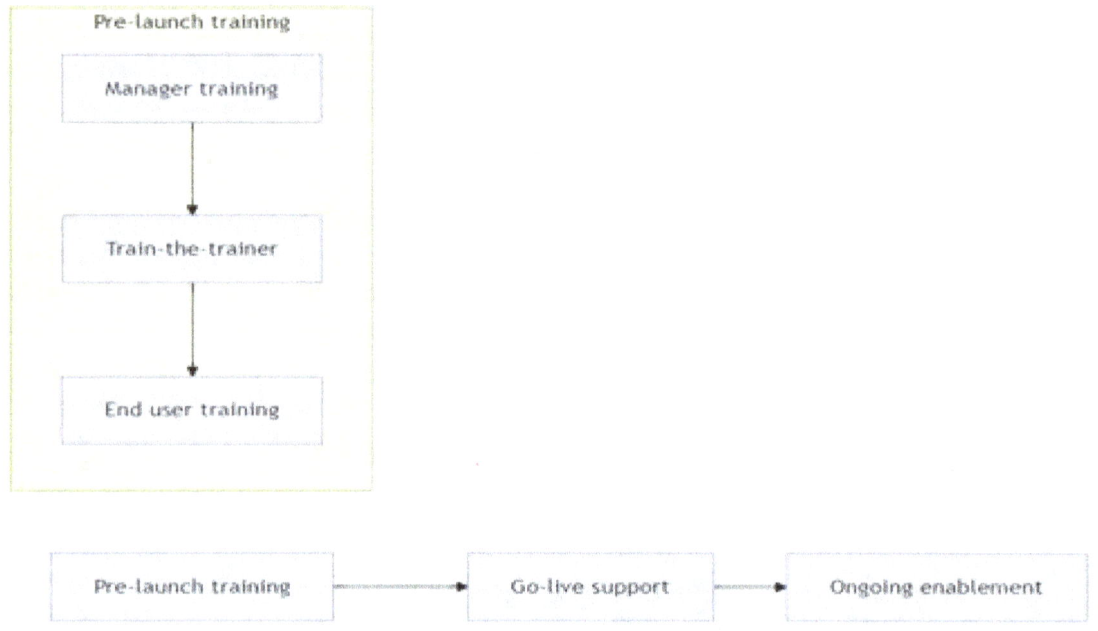

In this model, training begins before the system goes live with role-based courses for managers, power users (train-the-trainers), and end users. At go-live, a command center and hypercare support model provide high-touch assistance during the critical transition period. Once things stabilize, ongoing training and resources enable continuous learning.

4.4.2 Support Model

Even with thorough training, users will inevitably have questions and encounter issues as they use the new HRIS. Having a robust support model is essential to maintaining productivity and user satisfaction.

A typical HRIS support model includes:

- **Tiered support**: Issues are triaged and escalated based on complexity and urgency. Tier 1 handles common questions and basic troubleshooting, Tier 2 tackles more complex issues, and Tier 3 involves HRIS experts and vendor support for advanced problems.

- **Multiple channels**: Users should have various ways to get help, such as a self-service knowledge base, chatbot, email, phone, or in-person support. Different users prefer different channels.

- **SLAs**: Set and communicate service level agreements for response and resolution times based on issue severity. For example, critical issues that prevent users from performing core job functions should be addressed within an hour, while minor issues may have a 24-hour SLA.

- **Issue tracking**: Use a ticketing system to log, categorize, and track issues from report to resolution. This provides accountability and helps identify trends for proactive improvement.

- **Feedback loop**: Solicit user feedback on the support experience and use it to continuously refine the support model. Conduct regular surveys or user interviews to gauge satisfaction and gather ideas.

Here's a simplified diagram of a tiered HRIS support model:

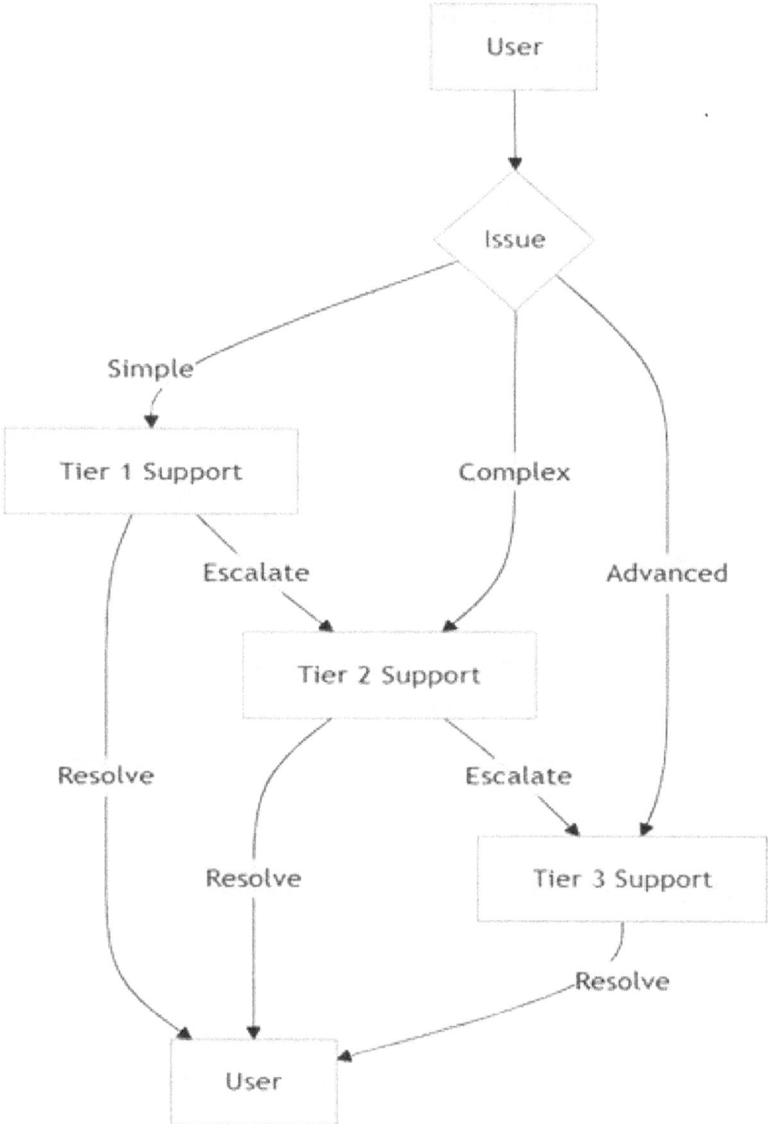

In this model, user issues are triaged based on complexity and routed to the appropriate support tier for resolution. Issues are escalated up the tiers as needed until they are resolved to the user's satisfaction.

The key is to design a support model that is user-centric, responsive, and geared towards continuous improvement. The HRIS team should work closely with HR and IT to ensure support processes are integrated and aligned with broader organizational goals.

4.4.3 Continuous Improvement

Your HRIS is not a static system. It should evolve over time to keep pace with changing business needs, new technologies, and user feedback. Continuous improvement is about proactively identifying and implementing enhancements to keep your HRIS fresh, relevant, and value-adding.

Some key aspects of continuous HRIS improvement include:

- **Usage analysis**: Monitor system usage metrics to understand how users are interacting with the HRIS. Look for bottlenecks, underutilized features, and areas of high demand. Use this data to prioritize improvements.

- **User feedback**: Actively solicit user feedback through surveys, focus groups, and ongoing dialogue. Understand what's working well, what's frustrating, and what new capabilities users want. Involve users in design and testing of enhancements.

- **Benchmarking**: Stay attuned to HRIS industry trends and best practices. Attend conferences, join user groups, and network with peers to learn how other organizations are using and improving their HRIS. Use this insight to benchmark your own system and processes.

- **Roadmap planning**: Maintain a living roadmap of planned HRIS improvements. Prioritize based on business value, user demand, and feasibility. Communicate the roadmap to stakeholders and provide regular progress updates.

- **Agile delivery**: Embrace an agile approach to HRIS enhancements. Break improvements into small, incremental releases that can be delivered quickly and iterated upon based on feedback. This allows for faster time-to-value and reduces the risk of large, disruptive changes.

Here's an example of an agile HRIS improvement cycle:

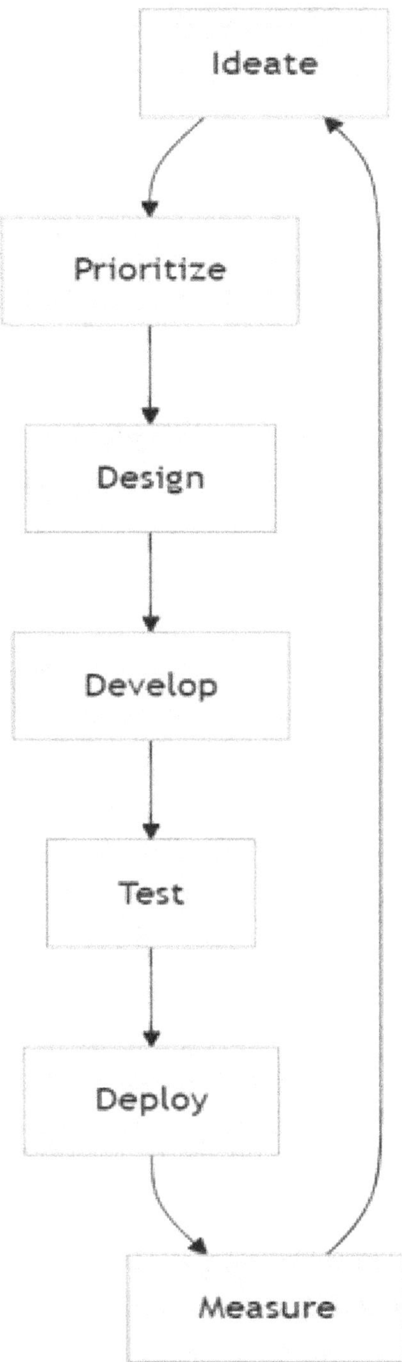

In this cycle, improvement ideas are continuously gathered and prioritized based on value and feasibility. High-priority items move into design and development, followed by testing and deployment. The impact of each improvement is measured and fed back into the ideation process for the next cycle.

By embedding continuous improvement into your HRIS operations, you ensure the system remains a valuable, strategic asset for your organization. It becomes a living, evolving platform that adapts to meet the ever-changing needs of HR and the broader business.

Conclusion

The post-implementation phase is where the rubber meets the road for your HRIS. By focusing on user training, support, and continuous improvement, you set your organization up for long-term success with the system.

Effective training ensures users are equipped to leverage the full power of the HRIS. A robust support model provides the assistance users need to stay productive and satisfied. And a continuous improvement mindset keeps the HRIS aligned with evolving business needs and user expectations.

Ultimately, the goal is to make the HRIS an integral part of your HR operations and employee experience. By investing in post-implementation activities, you maximize the value of your HRIS and position HR as a strategic partner to the business.

Conclusion

The journey through this book, *Architecting AI-Driven HRIS Solutions: Scalable Design, Project Management, and Quality Assurance for the Modern Enterprise,* has underscored the transformative potential of AI-driven Human Resource Information Systems (HRIS). The chapters have equipped readers with a comprehensive understanding of system architecture, strategic planning, project management, and quality assurance for HRIS implementation. This conclusion synthesizes the lessons learned, reflects on the future trajectory of HRIS, and highlights actionable insights for building resilient and scalable solutions.

The Evolving Landscape of AI-Driven HRIS

HRIS solutions have transcended their traditional roles as static repositories of employee data. The infusion of artificial intelligence, machine learning, and predictive analytics has elevated HRIS to strategic enablers of organizational growth. AI-driven HRIS now provides actionable insights into workforce trends, streamlines recruitment, personalized employee engagement, and optimizes performance management.

Discussion: One of the most notable advancements is the shift from transactional systems to decision-support systems. For example, AI-driven HRIS can predict employee turnover by analyzing factors like engagement scores, workload patterns, and career trajectories. These insights empower HR teams to proactively address attrition risks and foster a more engaged workforce.

- **Key Takeaway**: Organizations must embrace continuous learning and adaptation to stay ahead in this rapidly evolving space. Investing in AI capabilities, robust data pipelines, and integration with third-party systems will remain critical to achieving these goals.

Lessons Learned: Building Scalable and Resilient HRIS

Building an AI-driven HRIS is a complex endeavor, but the principles outlined in this book provide a foundation for success. The following lessons capture the essence of the discussions across chapters:

1. Scalability is Non-Negotiable

Designing for scalability is essential to accommodate growth in user base, data volume, and feature requirements. This involves leveraging cloud-native architectures, modular microservices, and elastic storage solutions.

- **Example**: A retail enterprise with a seasonal workforce can benefit from an HRIS that scales payroll processing capacity during peak seasons. Cloud platforms such as AWS or Azure enable on-demand resource allocation to meet these dynamic needs.

2. Data Integrity Drives AI Effectiveness

AI algorithms rely on high-quality data to deliver actionable insights. Ensuring data integrity through effective cleansing, validation, and governance practices is paramount.

- **Reflection**: Without reliable data, AI insights become noise rather than actionable guidance. Implementing automated data quality checks and auditing processes can mitigate this risk.

3. User-Centric Design Encourages Adoption

An HRIS, no matter how advanced, is only as effective as its adoption rate among employees and managers. Intuitive interfaces, mobile accessibility, and responsive support channels are critical for widespread acceptance.

- **Future Possibility**: Incorporating voice-enabled features and AI-driven chatbots could further enhance user engagement by providing immediate assistance and reducing learning curves.

The Role of Strategic Leadership

Leadership plays a pivotal role in the success of HRIS projects. Visionary leaders not only champion technology adoption but also foster a culture that embraces innovation and adaptability.

Discussion: Strong leadership bridges the gap between technical teams and business stakeholders, ensuring alignment on objectives and priorities. For instance, leadership can advocate for AI-driven HRIS by demonstrating ROI through pilot projects, such as automating repetitive tasks like resume screening or payroll calculations.

- **Real-World Application**: In one global organization, leadership's decision to pilot AI in performance management resulted in a 20% increase in employee satisfaction scores due to more personalized and transparent feedback processes.

Future of AI-Driven HRIS

The future of HRIS lies at the intersection of AI, blockchain, and edge computing. Organizations must anticipate and embrace these trends to remain competitive.

1. AI-Enhanced Personalization

HRIS systems will increasingly leverage AI to provide hyper-personalized experiences for employees. From tailored learning recommendations to personalized wellness initiatives, AI will redefine employee engagement.

- **Scenario**: An AI-driven HRIS could monitor an employee's workload and suggest mindfulness breaks or recommend reskilling courses based on career aspirations.

2. Blockchain for Data Security

Blockchain technology can revolutionize how HRIS systems manage sensitive employee data. By enabling secure and transparent data exchanges, blockchain ensures compliance with stringent regulations like GDPR.

- **Example**: A blockchain-enabled HRIS could allow employees to control access to their personal data, enhancing trust and privacy.

3. Edge Computing for Real-Time Analytics

As organizations become increasingly distributed, edge computing will allow HRIS systems to process data closer to the source. This will enable real-time decision-making, particularly in dynamic environments like retail or manufacturing.

- **Future Possibility**: Imagine an edge-enabled HRIS providing instant performance feedback to a manager during a shift, allowing for immediate recognition or coaching.

Actionable Insights for Practitioners

The insights presented in this book culminate in actionable recommendations for HRIS practitioners:

1. **Adopt a Phased Approach**: Start with core functionalities and scale incrementally to manage complexity and reduce risks.

2. **Invest in Training and Change Management**: Equip employees with the knowledge and confidence to embrace the new system.

3. **Prioritize Integration**: Ensure seamless connectivity with legacy systems and third-party platforms to maximize the value of AI-driven HRIS.

4. **Focus on Data Governance**: Establish robust policies to maintain data accuracy, security, and compliance.

5. **Collaborate Across Teams**: Foster partnerships between HR, IT, and leadership to align goals and drive collective success.

Conclusion

The journey of architecting AI-driven HRIS solutions is both challenging and rewarding. As organizations strive to build resilient, scalable, and user-centric systems, the principles and strategies outlined in this book serve as a guiding light. By embracing the transformative power of AI and fostering a culture of innovation, enterprises can unlock new dimensions of efficiency, engagement, and strategic value. The future of HRIS is bright, and the possibilities are endless—if approached with vision, discipline, and a commitment to excellence.

www.ingramcontent.com/pod-product-compliance
Lightning Source LLC
Chambersburg PA
CBHW081339160726
48000CB00010B/3167